NEW FOREST
FOLKLORE, TRADITIONS & CHARMS

PUBLISHED AVALONIA LTD

ISBN: 978-1-910191-29-3 (PAPERBACK)

NEW FOREST: FOLKLORE, TRADITIONS & CHARMS,
COPYRIGHT VIKKI BRAMSHAW, © 2022

COVER ART BY HELOISA SAILLE, © 2021

DESIGNED AND PRODUCED BY AVALONIA LTD
BM AVALONIA, LONDON, WC1N 3XX, UNITED KINGDOM
WWW.AVALONIABOOKS.COM

NEW FOREST

Folklore, Traditions & Charms

VIKKI BRAMSHAW

PUBLISHED BY AVALONIA

WWW.AVALONIABOOKS.COM

For Charlie aged 5,
who knew all this already.

ACKNOWLEDGEMENTS

Enchanted Forest of my dreams,
This feeble pen to draw you tries,
But day by day new beauties you unfold,
Unto my futile wondering eyes.

The Enchanted Forest,
Gladys M Forbes

With huge thanks to the staff of Ringwood Library and the Christopher Tower Reference Library, who remained open and welcoming when they could during the pandemic. My thanks also to the New Forest District Council, the New Forest Parish Councillors, the Forestry Commission and representatives of the Verderers of the New Forest, who all corresponded with me via email during lockdown and met me for coffee and cake whenever we were allowed!

A special mention to my son Charlie, who accompanied me for much of my research and has always managed to give me some fresh perspective. Also, to the countless local people who have imparted their knowledge one way or another during my time on the Forest[1].

---

1 'on' the Forest is the generally accepted local terminology, rather than 'in' the Forest.

TABLE OF CONTENTS

INTO THE FURZE:
INTRODUCTION

In the heathlands... completely detached from other people. Here I can lose myself physically in a trackless waste ... renewing an unknown source of strength within myself. In the heather, I feel suspended between earth and sky, even heaven and hell.

Sybil Leek, A Fool & A Tree

The New Forest is both one of the most beautiful and vastly remote parts of the south coast. It is also diverse; to the south the Forest opens up to coastal beaches whilst to the north the moors are hilly and wild, its boundaries meeting with the sacred landscape of Wiltshire. The term 'Forest' can be misleading. It is true that some of the New Forest is covered with woodland, but not all of this is ancient – much of the wooded areas are managed inclosures for timber production. However, the vast acreage of the New Forest is heathland and described as 'open forest': sweeping expanses of grassland complemented with bracken, blankets of fragrant heather and rare flowers, with adjacent commons and timber inclosures. Framed by the River Avon to the west and the Solent to the east, the Forest is a place that has remained largely unchanged since 11th-century Norman Forest Law was introduced, with many aspects of life still managed much as they were then. The Forest is also immersed in tradition and folk knowledge compounded due to its relative isolation, a perpetual feature of a rural community; some of this knowledge is alive in the Forest today but much is in danger of being forgotten forever.

The spiny *furze* (gorse) is a feature all over the Forest, with its bright yellow flowers which can start to bloom as early as January. The furze is essential to the survival of the Forest stock in the late winter and the insect population throughout the year (in particular, bees and rare butterflies) and in the past was used as a folk-cure to treat jaundice.[2] The New Forest also supports wetland flora and fauna that thrives in the unique ecosystem of bogland found right across the Forest. The more ancient woodlands of the Forest consist of holly, oak, beech, and silver birch, to name just a few, with foxglove, primrose and butcher's broom growing beneath their boughs. Holly is particularly important to Forest stock, both as a winter forage and something to rasp their teeth against; the deer do this too, leaving their mark on the trunks. The ponies also enjoy chewing on the ivy and honeysuckle which creep up tree trunks.

In the winter, the Forest can seem bleak and foreboding; low-lying clouds and sweeping flisky rain drives against the Forest stock, the ponies and cattle which call this 140,000-acre Forest their home. Intuitively knowing the best way to stay warm, they stand with their backs to the furze, bottoms tucked up and using their rubbery lips and front teeth to tentatively nibble at the young thorny shoots and tiny yellow flowers. The moors are covered in shades of dark orange and mahogany browns of bracken broken by grey and black hues of wintering heather, some of which has died right back, leaving pale grey skeletons behind like miniature trees from a tiny fairy world. Heather and gorse cover the vast majority of the open forest, together with yellow-green lawns which lie damp like soggy sponges in the winter. The holly in the Forest remains a rich green at this time of year with bright red berries, *'kind holly'* being the preferred pickings for the ponies.

> *Heather is never only heather,*
> *As moor is never merely moor.*
>
> From: The Lost Words, A Spell Book
> Robert Macfarlane & Jackie Morris

In the spring, the early morning frost burns off the moors as the sun warms the ground, covering the rolling landscape with an effect like dry ice that curls around the heather and gorse surrounded with tiny yellow tormentil blooms by May. The tops of the trees in the distance emerge from the mist as if from a liminal world above the clouds. There is nothing like a spring

---

2 The Pattern Under The Plough: George Ewart Evans

morning in the New Forest, thousands of waking birds bursting into song, and the hot breath of the cattle visible in the air as they move out into the moors. For those who are patient enough, tiny newts can be seen lurking at the bottom of clear shallow streams and toads laying their spaghetti-strings of eggs amongst the water weed. If you have keen eyesight you might spot an adder warming itself in the sun, its zig-zag pattern running the length of its body and blending in with the bracken. They hibernate in rodent burrows and fallen trees through the colder months, but by spring they have emerged and can occasionally be found basking on the mounds of *emmets* (a local term for ants) which are found in their dozens spread out over the greens. Each grassy mound is created by a single meadow ant colony, which builds up the hillock and fertilises the plants growing on top to create insulation and protection, with one flatter side facing south-east to capture the morning sun.[3] These hillocks were quite accurately described by Crespigny & Hutchinson as 'grass-grown buried cities'[4] and associated with the fairies. It is also considered unlucky to destroy the mounds; Gemma Gary writes that in Cornwall, ants (known there as *muryans*) are believed to be piskies or the old gods, which have become diminished in size.[5] By mid-May the bumble bees are busy on the holly bloom, the swifts are busy with their nests, and a small number of quality purebred stallions are released across the New Forest. It is always wise to keep your distance from the Forest stock but even more so at this time of the year, which is cause for much excitement for the mares as the stallions round them up into groups and defend them against rivals.

In the height of summer, the furze rattles. It can be a strange thing to experience for the first time, if you are sat quietly in the sunshine and suddenly hear the moor come alive with a sound that is something in between the buzz of a thousand bees and the rattle of a snake's tail. The sound is, in fact, the seed pod bursting and firing out its tiny little seeds into the air. The heather too

---

3 Lymington-Keyhaven Nature Reserve
4 The New Forest, Its Traditions, Inhabitants and Customs: De Crespigney & H Hutchinson
5 Traditional Witchcraft, A Cornish Book of Ways: Gemma Gary

crunches and releases its seeds as the Forest animals walk through its fragrant blooms. The smell of the Forest in the summer is glorious; an organic, dusty and sandy sort of smell, often with a salty hint of the ocean when a summer breeze is blowing from Lymington. The lawns at this time of year are hard as concrete and seemingly barren as brickdust, yet tiny little flowers endure such as yellow birdsfoot trefoil pushing up towards the sunshine, determinedly springing back up if trampled. During July and August you may spot the silver-studded blue butterfly – a tiny and exceptionally rare insect which can be found on the open heaths. Despite their rarity, if you are lucky enough to find them you will find your ankles surrounded by hundreds, a silver-blue haze of iridescent wings fluttering just a few inches above the heather.

As we draw towards the autumn the Forest starts to become more multi-toned. The heather turns to a deep purple, a blanket of the most gorgeous velvet fabric thrown over the landscape. The bracken and tree leaves turn to browns, oranges and reds - some years, it seems this change happens almost overnight. As the leaves start to fall, so do the acorns and here come the pigs to hoover them up, their ever-enthusiastic rootling and snuffling sounds complementing the orchestra of the autumn woodland. The ponies too become more active at this time of the year. Feeling well from the summer, they charge about with tails up, kicking out at the air and fresh with the hint of cooler weather. As autumn closes in on winter, one of my favourite events is the deer rut. Where we live we are surrounded by a large population of deer, and much of the winter they wander up and down our driveway, past my window and into the back of the garden. Then from November, the testosterone-driven young bucks come together to square each other up; the sound is extraordinary as they clash and lock antlers followed by the destruction of the undergrowth as they wrestle in the dark.

The landscape of the Forest has fulfilled my need for escapism and solitude since I was a child; its very essence nurtures a sense of power and freedom that can be felt in the bones. I am lucky enough to call the New Forest my home; for many years I have explored this landscape both on foot and by horse. Four feet are better than two and cover more ground, allowing me to explore further than I could otherwise manage. As a result, I have traversed this liminal and magical landscape, been silent within its noise, become acutely aware of its unique *genii loci* (spirits of place) and met so many interesting and knowledgeable characters along the way. I have also been lucky enough to get involved in different capacities with commoning on the New Forest, gaining a first-hand insight into this ancient tradition. I feel privileged not only to live and work in this Forest but to have been presented with a number of synchronistic opportunities to learn more about its history, lore and superstitions. I hope I have been able to convey these from the unique perspective of the New Forest itself, whilst also presenting comparisons and conjectures from traditions found in similar environments across the British Isles.

Finally, readers will become aware that this book covers the history of hunting in the New Forest and associated topics. The subject of hunting will be very emotive to many, but it was impossible to write this book without it. The New Forest was re-purposed as a Royal Hunting Ground from at least 1079 (if not before), and its landscape, customs and economy were all built around or affected by the Royal Hunt in some way. My aim is to simply make an account of this landscape's history where relevant to my primary subject of folklore, traditions and charms, many of which originate from a period of time very different to our own.

The traditions and lore of the Forest are fragile; this book is my contribution towards their preservation for future generations.

Vikki Bramshaw,
Summer 2021

ANCIENT HISTORY
OF THE FOREST

A PLACE BEFORE TIME

The New Forest lies within the Hampshire Basin, shaped by a relationship with water and ice over millions of years. It is a remarkable landscape, particularly in the north of the Forest, which is made up of rolling hillsides and vast swathes of open moorland and ancient woodlands, sunken valleys and epic ridgeways. The evidence of its watery origins can be found here, its curves and lines caused by the alternate locking up and release of water during fluctuating climates. The oldest evidence of this process are the sands and clays from the Eocene period, a huge period of time between 56-35 million years ago.[6] Here, we know the New Forest was exposed to considerably higher temperatures than today, and we find evidence of sub-tropical plants and creatures, such as the crocodile. As the climate fluctuated, for vast periods of time, much of the New Forest was underwater or otherwise warm and boggy. The earth reveals fossils from the Eocene period, such as sharks' teeth, snail shells and molluscs. Even coral has been found in abundance, such as a coral bed exposed during the building of a railway line between the villages of Brockenhurst and Sway.[7] Fossils are usually only found in the New Forest when freshly exposed during excavations or on cliff faces and riverbeds,[8] as the soil does not hold fossils for long once exposed.

On top of the sand and clay from the Eocene period we find flint river gravel, shining white on the heaths; my horse likes to shy away from these whenever possible, adding some excitement to my ride! The gravel is from our most recent Ice Age, a later period stretching from around 3 million - 10,000 years ago.

---

6 Timeline of the Ancient World: Chris Scarre
7 Geology of the New Forest: Ian West, Southampton University
8 Geology of the New Forest: Ian West, Southampton University

During this time Britain was exposed to a cycle of long periods of ice ages interspersed with shorter bursts of warmer climates each lasting about 20,000 years, known as interglacials.[9] The New Forest was a vast landscape of ice; without its own glaciers but in an ongoing state of permafrost and seasonal flooding, the white gravel washed down with thawing snow from neighbouring chalk hills or transported as deposits under snow travelling under its own weight.[10] Washed down with it were also discarded Palaeolithic objects such as axes and chopping tools with which our ancestors used to hunt European rhino, mammoth and reindeer, bison, deer and ponies.[11] There were also significant drops in sea levels as water became locked up in ice, which revealed land-bridges to places that were previously separated by water,[12] such as the English Channel, which at times was no more than a river. This area was explored by hunter-gatherers who crossed the valley, and many prehistoric artefacts lie under the Solent, now drowned by the sea.[13] The thawing of our most recent Ice Age began around 13,000 BCE. By 8,000 BCE, the environment was similar to ours today, and the New Forest was left as a landscape that had been formed and sculpted by the sea.

AFTER THE ICE

Despite the environment being a challenging one for human habitation, the watery origins of the New Forest have resulted in its protection as a unique ecosystem - specifically because it created large areas of boggy or unstable ground, underground springs and unfertile soil. However, there are parts of the Forest where the soil is underpinned by chalk, and it is here where we find valuable land which can be cultivated or developed. We also find a number of mineral-rich holy wells and springs known for their healing properties, particularly in the northern parts of the New Forest. These are a result of the iron-rich soil deposited by

---

9 Timeline of the Ancient World: Chris Scarre
10 Timeline of the Ancient World: Chris Scarre
11 H. Hutchinson: The New Forest
12 Timeline of the Ancient World: Chris Scarre
13 The New Forest Historical Landscape: Sue Davies, Karen Walker & Linda Coleman

the sea, and later in this book I will describe some of the sacred springs I have visited during my exploration of the New Forest.

Also in the north of the New Forest we find a soil known locally as the *red sands:* a reddish sand and clay which often preserves evidence of ancient plant materials.[14] The reddish colour is due to its high iron content, and ironstone, also known as 'Heathstone' or 'Hethstone', is also found here, created by the 'cementation' or hardening of the soil by iron-rich springs.[15] Strangely, this soil doesn't taste of blood as you might expect (yes, I have tasted it on numerous occasions and was disappointed each time, although it can mark the skin red for hours!) Sumner writes how the locals used to collect buckets of the red sands to layer the floor of their chicken coops and were known for the underside of their hens, which were always stained red.[16] As well as visible ironstone and sand deposits, we also often find fragments of ironstone turned up by badgers and foxes digging their sets and scattered across the surface. This ironstone is one of only two types of native New Forest stone, the other being *Burley Rock*.[17] Heathstone was quarried at Hasley Hill and elsewhere across the Forest by our ancient ancestors for building material, who may also have worked the stone as a crude iron-ore[18]. Iron would continue to be an important material both practically and magically, with simple charms such as iron horseshoes and nails being used to protect the home, as well as inside witch-bottles, where it was used as a form of counter-witchcraft and for other forms of local cunning magic.

> '*fragments of ironstone limonite … a natural product of sand indurated with iron … outside the eastern end of Hasley inclosure, there are extensive remains of rambling pits and hollows … that may have been made for obtaining ironstone, or heathstone as it is locally called.*'[19]

---

14 H. Hutchinson: The New Forest
15 Geology of the New Forest: Ian West, Southampton University
16 Heywood Sumner: A Winter Walk in the New Forest
17 Geology of the New Forest: Ian West, Southampton University
18 The Commoners New Forest: FE Kenchington
19 Heywood Sumner: A Winter Walk in the New Forest

Heathstone continued to be quarried until relatively recently, with leases issued giving permission to mine, and a fee charged based on the amount extracted.[20] The foundations of The Royal Oak pub at Fritham (dating from the 15th century) are composed of Heathstone that was probably sourced locally at Eyeworth.[21] Below the moors at Hasley we find the *Red Shoot Wood*, named after the hills behind them; the word 'shoot' meaning locally 'hill'. We also find the *white sands* in the north of the Forest, a powdery river deposit containing shells and other marine deposits. While on the subject of stone, a local geologist told me something very interesting to do with the rock under the north-westerly parts of the New Forest. Here exists a negative gravity anomaly; gravity is lower here than many other parts of Britain! The anomaly is probably caused by a mass of rock such as granite deep under the earth. You will be lighter and be able to jump higher in this region than many places elsewhere.[22]

THE NEW FOREST AND OUR ANCESTORS

'The same barrows still uplift their rounded forms on the plains; the same banks, the same entrenchments near which lived Kelt and Roman and Old-English, still run across the hills and valleys. The same churches rear their towers, the mills still stand by the same streams.' [23]

Palaeolithic New Forest (c.500,000 - 10,000 BCE)

It is during the Palaeolithic Age that we find the earliest evidence of our distant nomadic ancestors passing through the New Forest and gathering its resources. Late Upper Palaeolithic and early Mesolithic flint axes have been found at the Alderbury and Rockford gravel pits[24] and on open heathland at Godshill, Fritham and Matley. Rockford is almost completely eroded now due to the gathering of raw materials and natural erosion (and the fun had by generations of children running up and down in the sandy gravel!) In the southern parts of the Forest, evidence has

---

20 Lease documents held in the Christopher Towers Reference Library, Lyndhurst
21 New Forest Pottery Kilns & Earthworks: Anthony Pasmore
22 Ian West, Southampton University
23 John Richard de Capel Wise: The New Forest, Its History & Its Scenery
24 Heywood Sumner: The New Forest

been found around Brockenhurst village as well as dredged up onto the coastline by the Solent, all showing evidence of occupation by our ancient ancestors.[25]

Mesolithic New Forest (c.8,500 - 4,000 BCE)

It was during the warmer Mesolithic period that the English Channel was formed, separating Britain from the continent and establishing the coastline much as we know it today.[26] As the climate became milder and the Ice Age ended our Mesolithic ancestors worked flints in the Forest, suggesting they were hunting and gathering in the area;[27] they would have still been nomadic at this time, following seasonal resources. There have even been suggestions of animistic totems being created by the hunter-gatherers who once walked here. In the early 1900's, a Mr Auberon Herbert discovered pieces of flint in the New Forest, which he believed had been shaped by prehistoric man into human and animal forms. He published his finds in *The Times* in 1901, in an article named *The Early Man and His Stones*:

> *'...the stones are representations of the totems of the tribes ... the stones represented some animal or object which existed as the totem and had a sacred character ... Many of the stones may be holy stones, amulets or stones consecrated ... (and) cup stones used for sacrifices.'*

He described how they resembled suns, moons, fish, tusks, mountain peaks, animals and parts of the body. Although the theory is tempting, his claims are generally criticised, because it is believed the shapes of the flints he found are probably coincidental; his work remains unsupported.

Neolithic New Forest (c.4,000 – 2,400 BCE)

The Neolithic Age marked the beginning of small-scale farming and the domestication of animals, with people gradually beginning to settle in the area and clear areas of Forest for

---

25 The New Forest Historical Landscape: Sue Davies, Karen Walker & Linda Coleman
26 The New Forest Historical Landscape: Sue Davies, Karen Walker & Linda Coleman
27 Cultural Heritage of the New Forest: New Forest National Park Authority

farming.[28] We find evidence of their occupation and agricultural tools at Eyeworth, Furzehill, Gorley Hill and Rockford Common,[29] probably arriving by the River Avon and exploiting the richer soil north-west of the Forest. We also start to see the local people of the New Forest express their religious beliefs, an important theme of worship and commemoration expressed in the construction of barrows for their dead.[30]

In the New Forest we have several 'oval barrows' which are older than the more common round barrow and indicate mid-Neolithic/early Bronze graves, also used for burials. It's possible that the oval barrow was a transition from the older long barrow, which also housed bodies rather than cremations. Although much rarer in Hampshire, several Neolithic long barrows have survived in the immediate areas surrounding the New Forest such as *Giant's Grave*, a single 68m long barrow found at Breamore near Downton. The long barrow is accompanied by the *'Giants Chair'* bell barrow, not far from *Grim's Ditch* which, according to local folklore, was created by the devil (a word that from the 1200's referred to 'false' gods i.e., the old gods and land spirits of the British Isles).[31]

We also find huge earthworks in the surrounding area, such as Knowlton Henge, a late-Neolithic circular embankment where it is likely a circle of stone megaliths once stood. Local legend has it that in the 12th century the stones were broken up and reused for the church built in the centre of this sacred site. It is also surrounded by at least 40 barrows, two more earthen circles, and other prehistoric traces.[32]

Bronze Age New Forest (c.2,400 BCE - c.700 BCE)

It was at the very end of the Neolithic period and the start of the Bronze Age that we see the arrival of the Beaker culture in

---

28 The New Forest: H Hutchinson
29 Heywood Sumner: The New Forest
30 The New Forest Historical Landscape: Sue Davies, Karen Walker & Linda Coleman
31 Online Etymology Dictionary
32 Ancient Stones of Dorset: Peter Knight

Britain, around 2600-1800 BCE. It is believed that they had a hand in the acceleration of farming techniques and trading in Britain and, as the New Forest entered the Bronze Age, there was an explosion in agriculture, especially around the edges of the Forest where the soil was richer. However, with the good comes the bad and the increase of farming quickly exhausted the already poor soil of the New Forest. According to a study published by the New Forest Park National Authority, it was at this time that the already poor soil became all but exhausted by the intensive farming, and heathland began to appear in its place.[33] But it was the search of metals that probably brought the so-called Beaker people to our shores. Named after the bell-shaped pottery typical of their style, the Beaker culture spread to Britain from Europe by way of a combination of both physical migration of people and the adoption of Beaker culture by native Britons. The Beaker pottery style was manufactured into drinking cups and vessels for other liquids, such as for smelting metals, and in Britain, many examples of their pottery show that they were used as cremation urns. The Beaker DNA significantly added to the British gene pool, and some research suggests that it may have almost completely overtaken that of the previous Neolithic inhabitants of Hampshire.

The Bronze Age also marked a significant increase in major settlements, especially in the northern valleys (such as those of Ellingham and Hucklesbrook)[34] , probably due to their position on the River Avon. On the other side of the Forest, to the northeast at Testwood Lakes, the remains of a Bronze Age oak wooden jetty or bridge has been discovered with a bronze Rapier (short sword) driven into the silt below. Finds such as this are often considered to be offerings to the gods or a sacrificial tool; this may well be the case here. Just as pins or other fine metalware

---

33 Cultural Heritage of the New Forest: New Forest National Park Authority
34 The New Forest Historical Landscape: Sue Davies, Karen Walker & Linda Coleman

were snapped or bent during the act of sorcery,[35] the destruction of weapons was part of sacrificial magic.

We also start to see the use of major ancient trackways across the Forest at this time. Many of these were wide enough for carts to use and connected major settlements, moving goods and livestock from place to place.[36] In old records we find New Forest trackways referred to as 'kingsways', 'horse roads', 'great roads' and 'old ways.'[37] One such major trackway is Hampton Ridge, a favourite of mine where I have spent many a windswept morning with a reluctant animal accompanying me. Locally known as *Snake Road*, the route connected the Gorley Common settlement to Fritham and beyond to Southampton.[38] This trackway is also locally known as *Old Shutt*.[39] It is generally understood that *Shutt* is from Shoot/Shute for 'a steep inclined plain or hillside track', which is generally correct. A similar name can be found in the nearby *'Red Shoot'* woods, at the back of a high ridge with red sand/clay soil.[40] However, in this case, according to local lore, the name Shutt refers to the effect of the incline upon a horse in traces attempting to climb the hill. The person driving would have to get out and put his own weight on the front of the shafts to prevent the windpipe of the horse being 'shut' i.e., closed.[41] Many of the smaller tracks are equally ancient, some being no more than pony paths worn over many hundreds of years. These are sometimes known as *fairy paths* or *spirit tracks* and many are also leys.

35 Traditional Witchcraft, A Cornish Book of Ways: Gemma Gary
36 The Folklore of Hampshire & the Isle of Wight: Wendy Boase
37 The Ancient Earthworks of the New Forest: Heywood Sumner
38 The Ancient Earthworks of the New Forest: Heywood Sumner
39 Wanderers in the New Forest, Juliette de Bairacli Levy
40 The New Forest, Heywood Sumner
41 Ann Sevier, Chair of Hyde Parish Council & New Forest District Councillor

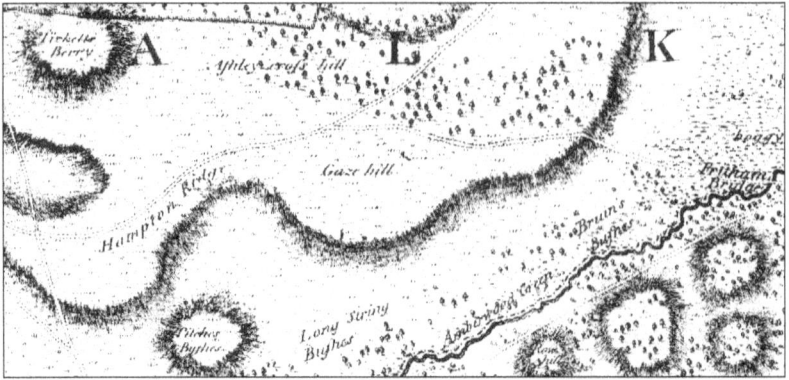

HAMPTON RIDGE, 1789 DRIVERS MAP

As cultural behaviours started to develop, so we see an acceleration in religion and spirituality. There are literally hundreds of intact Bronze Age barrows or *'butts'* in the New Forest, including round barrows, bell barrows and disc barrows. Locally, barrows were known to be *'Burial Places of Giants'*, with giants responsible for their construction and fairies or other supernatural beings known to be living within them.[42] Seven barrows found together were known to be particularly associated with fairies. Some even had their very own legends about them, such as one known as *Cold Pix's Cave* on Beaulieu Common, which is haunted by the *Colt Pixy*. A common position for *butts* in the New Forest was above bogs and valleys. This can be seen all over the Forest, but my particular favourites are those at Setley and near Hampton Ridge. They are also found following (or overlooking) rivers and tributaries, such as one of the barrows at Rockford Common, which stands on the very top of the hill and overlooks the River Avon and beyond. It's unlikely there was a settlement here, but that they were connected to the nearby Castle Piece Camp at Roe Wood.[43] Certainly their position overlooking water will have had some connection to the transient liminality of water and marshland, a veil between this world and the other, a fitting place for burial as well as, perhaps, the marking of territories and land ownership. In several places in the New Forest barrow sites can be found named as *'castles'*, with Browns

---

42 The Folklore of Hampshire & the Isle of Wight: Wendy Boase
43 The Ancient Earthworks of the New Forest: Heywood Sumner

Castle on Ibsley Common perhaps an example of this. Sumner writes that the presence of Bronze Age barrows on plains adjoining bodies of water (such as those near Beaulieu River) may also suggest that the more fertile land that supported these societies now lies beneath the Solent.[44]

To the casual eye, New Forest barrows are often not always obvious. Unlike the neighbouring counties of Wiltshire and Dorset, barrows are often concealed by wild scrub and vegetation, and many have collapsed due to erosion because of the poor soil or plough-out. Many have also suffered amateur excavation, a popular pastime in the 18th & 19th centuries and have holes or dips in the middle as a result - there are several New Forest tales of buried treasure within barrows, which may have fuelled the interest to excavate these sites! For instance, the barrows at Copythorne, locally known as *Money Hills*, are said to contain treasure, and in the early 19th century one of the barrows near Fritham village was opened up by a local man who *'constantly dreamed that he should find there a crock of gold.'*[45] The connection between mounds and treasure is a reoccurring one; in Cornwall it is believed that a piece of tin buried inside an ants hillock would transform into silver.[46]

We will never know what treasures were found in many of the opened barrows, as their contents were often claimed by the finders and never recorded. But those that were recorded have revealed ashes and urns with accompanying grave goods for use in the next world, such as weapons and coins. The round barrow at Shirley Holms near Sway is dated circa 2000-1500 BCE and held an urn and ashes, whilst nearby the rare 'twin-disc barrows' at Setley, dated circa 1600-1200 BCE, were found to hold a cremation with 'parcels' of burnt earth, wood and charcoal. However no urn was found here, suggesting this might have been an offering site rather than a grave. There are three 'disc barrows' on the site with two intersecting, creating the twin. Heywood

---

44 The Ancient Earthworks of the New Forest: Heywood Sumner
45 The Folklore of Hampshire & the Isle of Wight: Wendy Boase
46 Traditional Witchcraft, A Cornish Book of Ways: Gemma Gary

Sumner describes the central mounds as the 'sacred area' of the barrow.[47] A similar-shaped site has recently been discovered and excavated by archaeologists at the Beaulieu Estate. Here, a Bronze Age monument was uncovered, comprising a similar ring ditch with entrance-way, suggesting not only a burial site but also a ritual meeting space. This site revealed five Bronze Age cremation urns, together with evidence of earlier Mesolithic people (a rare find for the New Forest), demonstrating how important this site might have been to our ancestors.[48] Another notable site is Stagbury Hill Barrow Cemetery, near Bramshaw. The Stagbury mound is likely to be a natural formation, but one that has been used by settlers for thousands of years for different purposes. There are four surviving barrows at the top of the mound (both round barrows and bell barrows, circa 1500-1100 BCE) and many more surrounding it. There may well have been more barrows on the mound; however it has suffered a great deal of erosion over the years, including being used as a pillow mound (medieval rabbit warren) in the medieval period. The summit of Stagbury is one of the highest points in the Forest, and as such is a fitting place for the burials of important individuals who could survey their territories from here in the afterlife. Foxhill Barrow Cemetery is also worth mentioning, being the largest known tumuli site in the New Forest and the site of at least 11 surviving barrows.

It is worth noting that there are many other interesting formations found on the Forest, such as the earth-banks of animal enclosures and *Bee Garns* to keep livestock out.[49] We have to be careful not to misidentify these sorts of earthworks for older archaeological sites; happily they are really interesting in their own right. Other earthworks are legacies of WW2: on Black Heath in Linwood, a number of pits and circular earthworks resembling disc barrows are scattered on the hill overlooking the heath in one direction and farmland in the other. I chanced upon these

---

47 The Ancient Earthworks of the New Forest: Heywood Sumner
48 The Advertiser & Times, 20th November 2020
49 The New Forest, Its Traditions, Inhabitants and Customs: De Crespigney & H Hutchinson

earthworks during a walk, first suspecting them to be the relics of a settlement but subsequently advised by a local historian that the shapes are in fact the remains of a WW2 experimental searchlight area.[50] Whilst these remains are not ancient, the area was obviously of some importance in the past. The name *Black* suggests that this site may have been used for cremation or charcoal burning in the past, and specifically for the pottery kilns that created *New Forest Pottery* or *New Forest Ware* - the so-called *Clonmore Vase* was discovered a stones' throw from Black Heath during the excavation of a pottery kiln on the grounds of a private property in 1955.[51]

Boiling Mounds

Another Bronze Age feature of the New Forest are the Boiling Mounds or *Burnt Mounds* - crescent or kidney-shaped mounds of calcined (burnt) stone and charcoal, next to a water trough or hollow. There are over 300 boiling mound sites in the New Forest, with the majority dated to the Bronze Age and others to the later Iron Age. The stones would have been heated in a fire, dropped into the water to boil it, and then discarded, a process carried out over many years thereby creating the mounds. It is generally accepted that boiling mounds were used for cooking or other processing of food products and by-products such as tanning hides. Whilst just conjecture, another theory is that they may have been used for sweatlodge purposes.[52] The sweatlodge tradition was alive elsewhere in Europe in the Bronze Age[53] and used for purification, changing the participants' consciousness and communicating with the ancestors. It is particularly interesting that a piece of black fabric was found at one Boiling Mound site at Deadman Bottom; the fabric is identical to that found in a Bronze Age funeral urn found at Stoney Cross and it raises the question of why a cremation urn

---

50 Linwood Searchlight Site, New Forest Knowledge archive: R Reeves
51 The Proceedings of The Hampshire Field Club, Vol. XXXII Pt. 2, 1965
52 A Ritualistic Interpretation of Bronze-Age Burnt Mounds: Alex Loktionov, University of Cambridge
53 A Ritualistic Interpretation of Bronze-Age Burnt Mounds: Alex Loktionov, University of Cambridge

would have been present at a site used solely for the production of food.[54]

Iron Age New Forest (c.700 BCE - c.43 CE)

During the Iron Age, people continued to farm the open Forest, creating ditches and earthwork banks for boundaries and animal enclosures, some of which can still be seen today. As the population began to grow, defensive hillforts began to be built on higher ground, such as Castle Hill, situated on a plateau at the edge of Burley village overlooking the Forest. The name Burley may be a legacy of this hillfort; from the Old English *burh* (fortified place) and *leah* (clearing).

Another notable Iron Age settlement is Hengistbury Head, a coastal headland which juts out to sea from the Christchurch area, at the far most south-westerly reaches of the New Forest. Evidence of human habitation at Hengistbury Head has been found as early as the Mesolithic period, with excavations carried out at the so-called *Mesolithic Archers Campsite*, which revealed thousands of artefacts. It continued to be a site of importance to our ancestors into the Bronze Age, with a number of barrows found in the area, one being found to hold the cremation remains of a young woman laid with a number of grave goods ready for her to take into the afterlife. Indeed, the custom of burying the dead and their funerary wares in barrows continued into the early Iron Age in the New Forest; some examples exist at Hatchet Moor where a cart burial was discovered.[55] During the Iron Age, Hengistbury Head was a major ironworks and coastal trading port, with the River Stour and Avon used to transport goods inland.[56] Hengistbury Head would also become the stronghold for the *Durotriges*, an alliance of Celtic tribes who began inhabiting much of the south coast from around 400 BCE. The Durotriges held a number of dominant hill forts on the south coast and by 44 CE their territory may have extended as far east as the River

---

54 Boiling Mounds in the New Forest: AH Pasmore & J Pallister
55 Heywood Sumner: The New Forest
56 The New Forest Historical Landscape: Sue Davies, Karen Walker & Linda Coleman

Test and possibly as far west as Lyme Regis, with Poole Harbour being another major trading port.[57] Evidence shows their habitation included unique pottery and metalwork such as brooches, swords and the Durotriges Stater,[58] a coin made in the mint at Hengistbury Head. Durotriges are also identified by their form of crouched burial: a shallow oval grave sometimes lined with stone slabs, with heads positioned towards the East and laid to rest with grave goods such as food, pottery, jewellery and swords.[59]

The Durotrigian name may come from *duro* 'hard' and *trig* 'inhabitant' (meaning something like 'hilltop dweller') or possibly from *dour* or *dwr*[60] (referring to a body of water, or 'dwellers by the water'), derived perhaps from the River Test or their general proximity to the south coast and sea connections.[61] Those at Hengistbury Head actively resisted invasion, and as such it did not find itself under attack like other sites such as Maiden Castle in Dorchester.[62] The New Forest itself was a sub-territory of the Durotriges, with strongholds around the edge of the Forest including Frankenbury Hill Fort at Godshill (otherwise known as *Godmanes Cap*). At 11 acres, this was the largest hill fort in the area, and hoards of Durotrigian coins have been found here. Amongst other items, Frankenbury produced and traded pottery which was most likely crafted in the local area of the New Forest.

Other New Forest hillforts from the Iron Age period include Buckland Rings at Lymington, with a probable beacon on the other side of the river to the south-east called Windmill Nap (otherwise known as Mount Pleasant)[63] and Toothill, in Ower.

The Roman New Forest (43 CE - 410 CE)

Roman settlement sites are found around the periphery of the Forest, such as along the Avon Valley towards Salisbury and

---

57 The Search for the Durotriges: Martin Papworth
58 The Search for the Durotriges: Martin Papworth
59 The Search for the Durotriges: Martin Papworth
60 The Search for the Durotriges: Martin Papworth
61 The Search for the Durotriges: Martin Papworth
62 Heywood Sumner: The New Forest
63 Heywood Sumner: The Ancient Earthworks of the New Forest

Southampton,[64] as well as Lymington and the Isle of Wight making use of the local shipping and trading ports. The Isle of Wight, known to the Romans as *Vectis*, was also used as a strategic station for guarding the coastline and a 'jumping off point' for attacks on hostile vessels.[65] The most notable Roman settlement site on the fringes of the New Forest is Rockbourne, home to Rockborne Roman Villa near Fordingbridge. Rockbourne was previously a late Iron Age settlement later adopted by the Romans, and was likely an administrative centre to the pottery industry, which spread over a vast estate of probably around 20,000 acres. The Romans were keenly invested in the manufacture and trade of pottery in the area, utilising local workforces and materials. Kilns were generally in use c.250 CE - c.370 CE[66] producing reproductions of Roman jugs,[67] but also locally influenced designs, described by earlier writers such as H. Hutchinson as 'native pottery' known as the aforementioned *New Forest Pottery* that would be traded throughout Europe.[68] The pottery industry was active over at least three square miles of the north-western reaches of the New Forest, from Fordingbridge across to Fritham; most notably, evidence has been found at Sloden, Crock Hill, Islands Thorns and Ashley Rails. Sloden stands on a high vantage point near Hampton Ridge, which would have been a convenient transportation route. It was first excavated in the 1920's by the amateur archaeologist and author Heywood Sumner, with other excavations since revealing nine Romano British Pottery kiln spoil banks and pieces of pottery scattered all over the local area. Sloden has its own legends: according to local lore the Romans buried a calf made of gold

---

64 The New Forest Historical Landscape: Sue Davies, Karen Walker & Linda Coleman
65 The Folklore of Hampshire & the Isle of Wight: Wendy Boase
66 The New Forest Historical Landscape: Sue Davies, Karen Walker & Linda Coleman
67 The New Forest Historical Landscape: Sue Davies, Karen Walker & Linda Coleman
68 Heywood Sumner: The New Forest

here.[69] Sloden has also revealed boiling mounds, with later surveys confirming that it was an Iron Age hillfort.

Ytene: Land of the Jutes (410 – 1066CE)

The Jutes originated from Jutland in northern Denmark, with the Angles and the Saxons coming from northern Germany. Together all three peoples are loosely referred to as the Anglo-Saxons. Sailing along the coast, the Angles and Saxons took land further north and west while the Jutes took Kent, the Isle of Wight and Hampshire, extending to the western reaches of the New Forest. Evidence of their landing can be seen in various seafarers camps, such as at Ampress in Lymington.[70] We know that they were settling on New Forest shores by the late 4th century CE, a migration which largely occurred after the departure of the Romans; however the Jutes in the New Forest may have begun to arrive much earlier, as we know that the Forest was in most respects of little interest to the Romans.[71] Once they had become established in the area (a process that was more probably gradual than history generally recalls) the New Forest became known as Ytene - from *Yt* ('Jute') and *ene* ('inhabitant') a term that was still used as late as the 12th century.[72] According to legend, the Jutes were of remarkably large stature (the etymology of *Jute* suggesting *giant* or *monster*) and as such, folklore would know Ytene as the *land of the giants*. This might also point to why barrows in the New Forest are sometimes referred to as '*burial places of giants*'. Although the barrows in the New Forest pre-date the Jutes by far, according to Ronald Hutton[73] the Anglo-Saxons often reused old barrows rather than constructing their own; perhaps that also happened in the New Forest.

The Anglo-Saxons brought new skills and artistic approaches to our shores, particularly notable being their gold jewellery and

---

69 The Folklore of Hampshire & the Isle of Wight: Wendy Boase
70 The Ancient Earthworks of the New Forest: Heywood Sumner
71 The New Forest Historical Landscape: Sue Davies, Karen Walker & Linda Coleman
72 The New Forest Historical Landscape: Sue Davies, Karen Walker & Linda Coleman
73 Ronald Hutton: The Pagan Religions of the Ancient British Isles

elegant pottery. They also brought us the runes (an alphabet which would continue to be used in Britain for centuries after their arrival) and their language, which influenced the native tongue and local place-names, and is now referred to as Old English. The cult of Woden was also an important feature brought to Britain by the Anglo-Saxons. According to the legends recounted in the late 9th century *Anglo-Saxon Chronicle,* two brothers named *Hengist* and *Horsa* (descendants of Woden) led the Anglo-Saxons' migration into Britain. As well as being a tale about the Anglo-Saxons' physical arrival in Britain, it almost certainly also refers to the arrival of the cult of Woden, which became established here in Britain, despite Christianity having already taken root by 400 CE, and became interwoven with the ancient traditions and superstitions surrounding the old chthonic gods and land spirits of the British Isles.

Later, during the Saxon period, the culture and landscape of the Forest was further influenced by the establishment of Saxon churches and parishes. A number of settlements and farming communities existed here. This was not a 'wasteland', as the Forest is so often described, but a busy common land, with its own pre-existing commoning rights and almost certainly already in use as a hunting reserve well before the Norman invasion.[74]

---

74 The Common Lands of England and Wales: WG Hoskins & L Dudley Stamp

CREATION OF THE FOREST

He made a great refuge for his game,
Imposing laws about the same.

Anglo Saxon Chronicle

NOVA FORESTA

Today we usually associate the word Forest with an area thickly wooded with trees, but the original meaning of the word was quite different and from the Latin *foris* or *foresta* meaning 'out of doors' or 'open land' – thus, wild open ground, moors and plains. The word may also find its roots in the Welsh *gores* or *gorest* meaning gorse or furze.[75] The purpose of a 'Forest' was very specific in William the Conqueror's time: a tract of land set aside and managed for the purposes of the royal hunt and under his Forest Law, in a process known as *afforestation*, he declared in 1087 that Ytene be renamed *Nova Foresta,* the 'New Forest'. As Manwood describes it in 1598, it was:

> *'a territorie of wooddy grounds and pastures, privileged*
> *for wild beasts and foules of the forrest, chase and warren to*
> *rest and abide in, in the safe protection of the King for his*
> *princely delight and pleasure.'[76]*

As a Royal hunting ground, the New Forest was repurposed to revolve around blood sport for royalty, the pursuits of hawking and hunting. Forest Laws placed new restrictions on the hunting of game, the ancient *Beasts of Venery* or *Beasts of Chase* including any animal that was of Crown interest to hunt. These included deer, wild boar, pine marten (or 'marten cat'), fox and in some cases, the wolf. There were also the *Beasts of Warren* - the rabbit and hare, pheasant and partridge.[77] Occasionally a special quarry would be imported for the chase (one more recent example being

---

75 The Forest in Folklore & Mythology: Alexander Porteous
76 Manwood's Treatise of the Forest Laws (1598): John Manwood
77 The New Forest: Rose C De Crespigny & Horace Hutchinson

the release of a jackal 'of great ferocity' that was brought to the New Forest in 1850.)[78]

Forest Law restrictions had other implications for local people, such as the size of dog that was allowed to run unhindered within the boundaries of the Forest. This was enforced by the *Court of Regard,* which inspected all dogs at least every three years and employed a metal instrument known as the *Rufus Stirrup Iron.* Any dog too large to pass through the stirrup was barbarically lamed, by the declawing or removal of toes and heelpads with a chisel and mallet[79], referred to as *lawing* or *expeditation.* Smaller dogs were able to pass through the middle of the stirrup, therefore spared as they were not considered a threat to the King's game. A pseudo-relic replica of the stirrup can be seen at the New Forest Heritage Centre. Nor could you necessarily freely enclose your own land (and approved fencing was generally considered to fence *against* common grazing rather than the reverse)[80] or clear your own land for agriculture (an offence called *Assart*). Restrictions were also placed on cutting timber and cleaning of undergrowth (*Vert*);[81] perhaps here began the local New Forest legend that the man in the moon was sent there for stealing wood from the Forest. The theme of being banished to the moon for crimes related to cutting *vert* (wood, herbage and undergrowth) is common across the British Isles and beyond. A similar Black Forest tale from Germany describes how an unfortunate man stole a bundle of wood from the forest on a Sunday (when he knew the Foresters wouldn't be patrolling) and was banished to the moon by God.[82] The severity of punishment surrounding Forest Law varied depending on who was on the throne. It is said that during the reign of King John (1199-1216) a great number were executed for breaking Forest Laws and that

---

78 The Illustrated London News, April 27th 1850
79 Manwood's Treatise of the Forest Laws (1598): John Manwood
80 The Common Lands of England and Wales: WG Hoskins & L Dudley Stamp
81 Rose Crespigny & H. Hutchinson: The New Forest – Its Traditions, Inhabitants & Customs
82 The Forest in Folklore & Mythology: Alexander Porteous

his executioner at Odiham Castle, Cains Appulyarde, *'gave the thumbs of their fathers to their children to play with.'*[83]

For a long time it was suggested that the afforestation of Ytene caused a huge upheaval to the landscape, with a picture painted of thriving villages and agricultural communities depopulated and destroyed to create a vast expanse for the new hunting ground. The reality, however, was probably less dramatic. Although there is evidence of land value being drastically reduced during afforestation (including the value of manors and their estates, which would have had a knock-on effect on those employed in them), it's likely that the Forest was already being used as a hunting reserve for Saxon nobility before the Norman conquest and that due to the poor soil condition the area had always been sparsely populated, being largely unsuitable for agriculture. This is the natural state of the Forest, a fact supported by local names such as *Bratley* (brittle wood), *Netley Marsh* and *Matley* (both indicating wet land), those ending in *'lease'* (poor land) or those ending in *'more'* (marshland), not forgetting its ancient name *Ytene*, archaically, though incorrectly, thought to mean 'furzy waste'. Certainly, the Forest Laws themselves would have had a significant impact on the local people in the New Forest, but it is unlikely that the landscape and its population were physically devastated in the way history has generally suggested. Wise writes that during the afforestation about two-thirds of Ytene was afforested, but this was largely common land and woodland, with villages and more valuable farmland remaining untouched.[84] We do know that a number of community buildings were lost, such as the chapel that stood at Thorougham, a village near Beaulieu which once existed in the area of Park Farm. However several royal residences and hunting lodges were built at this time, and a number of estates established by wealthy landowners or aristocratic Lords favoured by the King continued to offer employment and leaseholds to local people.

---

83 A History of Hunting in Hampshire: Brig. Gen. JFR Hope
84 The New Forest, its History & its Scenery: JR Wise

Although Forest Law was at times an oppressive institution, in the long run it has preserved the character of the Forest by controlling development and exploitation. As hunting began to decline in the 15th century, the Crown's interest in the New Forest began to turn to using its timber to supply the shipping industry and navy. Timber was being cut in great swathes, with animals being turned out without rights and Forest Laws ignored. However, by the 1700's an enthusiasm was shown to replant the timber that had been lost and 300 acres of oaks were planted by Charles II, with another 6,000 acres by William III. By the 1800's, the organisation of the Forest was revisited and the byelaws and matters to do with commoning (such as specific rights and dates) were fixed.[85] As part of this change, in 1851 the Deer Removal Act was introduced. As hunting was no longer the main feature of the New Forest, the deer began to increase in great numbers. Not only were the deer experiencing sickness and lack of grazing due to their overpopulation, they were also taking a great deal of grazing from the commoners' animals, which were already suffering from loss of grazing due to the inclosure of ground for timber. As compensation, the Deer Removal Act was established which culled the deer to more manageable numbers. This suited the commoners, despite another 10,000 acres of land being enclosed after the Act was carried out! In response, another Act was passed in 1877 which ensured that no more than 16,000 acres of land could be enclosed for timber. The Forest Laws of *Winter Heyning* and *Fence Month* (periods of time when commoners stock should be removed from the Forest for the benefit of the deer) was also done away with, as it was now irrelevant.[86]

The New Forest today accommodates 16,000 acres of timber inclosures, largely Scots Pine. Although the pine is enclosed, the trees don't know that; the quick-growing Scots Pine throws its seeds far in the wind, quickly encroaching on the surrounding moors and jeopardising the long-term ecosystem and character of the New Forest.

---

85 The New Forest, its History & its Scenery: JR Wise
86 The New Forest: Rose C De Crespigny & Horace Hutchinson

BEATING THE BOUNDS & PERAMBULATIONS

In ancient times the boundaries of the New Forest were fluid, adjusting to changes in power and local administration, and were first defined by natural formations such as the rivers to the east and west, the sea to the south and the chalk to the north. The boundaries came to be recorded by *perambulation*, or survey, taken at that time by foot and on horseback, attended by Forester officials and representatives of the Crown[87] and in some cases, Knights such as those listed in King Henry's perambulation of 1218: *'by the Knights subscribing* ... (list of 33 knights) *who say on the Bible that these are the boundaries of the New Forest.'* A perambulation would follow certain landmarks such as hedges and bushes, *'the bush called Wynnatesbush growing in the common road of Markway'* (1215)[88] and large trees, for example *'a certain oak called Markoake'* (1670).[89] It also followed ditches, earthen mounds, marlpits, stones and posts, for example *'decayed post'* (1670).[90] Later perambulations also mention private estates and parks. Many boundary stones and posts still exist in some fashion and show the boundaries between parishes, although others can now only be seen on old Driver maps.

The tradition of *Beating the Bounds* was often an integral part of boundary surveys across the British Isles. As the perambulation stopped at various points, the boundary landmark would be struck with a willow walking stick. Accounts are also made of local boys being struck where a boundary had been encroached or a bowerstone moved.[91] Not only did the Beating of the Bounds show where the boundaries were, they also had ceremonial significance, with rapping the staff thought to drive away evil or disturb negative spirits. Walking the route was also a powerful process in itself, defining control of an area and possibly even

---

87 See 1297 Edward I Perambulation (Christopher Tower Library)
88 Perambulation 1215 Christchurch Cartulary (Christopher Tower Library)
89 Calendar of New Forest Documents 15th-17th centuries: DJ Stagg (Perambulation 1670)
90 Calendar of New Forest Documents 15th-17th centuries: DJ Stagg (Perambulation 1670)
91 The Folklore of Hampshire & the Isle of Wight: Wendy Boase

considered as drawing power from the land. George Ewart Evans writes that this custom finds its origins in the Roman festivals of Terminalia and Ambarvalia, which reaffirmed perambulations whilst also driving away evil from the boundaries.[92] The custom was continued here in the British Isles, although possibly the reason why was lost to most. Although at the time of my research I found no record of any such customs in the New Forest, it is more than possible that similar boundary customs existed here.

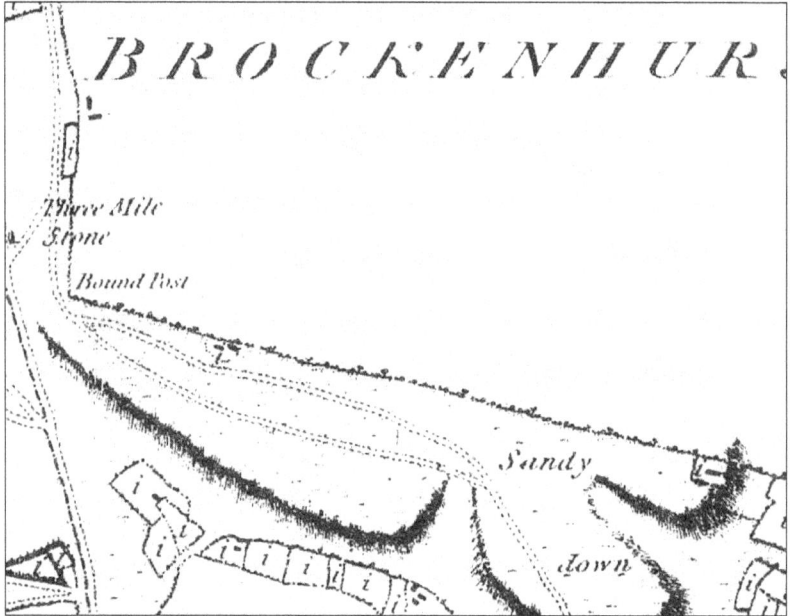

THREE MILE STONE AND BOUND POST, BROCKENHURST (1789 DRIVERS MAP)

92 The Pattern Under the Plough: George Ewart Evans

NEW FOREST COMMONING: TRADITIONS & FOLKLORE

COMMONING & ITS HISTORY

Once widespread across the British Isles, commoning provided various rights on common land such as the grazing of cattle and arable farming (like haymaking) and could be found on small village greens and large tracts of landscape alike. Common land was often managed by large estates, granted by the Crown to local aristocratic Lords who in turn would oversee the rights of common. Today, only a small proportion of common land in Britain is used for this traditional purpose, with most repurposed as recreational grounds with the 'right to roam'.

As a Royal Hunting Ground, the commoning allowed in the New Forest during Norman rule was largely dictated by Forest Law, which first and foremost protected the Kings interest in the vert and venison (*vert:* woods, herbage and undergrowth and *venison:* game animals, specifically deer as quarry for sport). As such, arable commoning was not permitted. However the rights of grazing cattle, ponies and occasionally sheep (*Common of Pasture*), turning out pigs for at least 56 days in the autumn (*Common of Mast*), gathering wood for fuel (*Right of Estovers*), cutting peat for fuel (*Right of Turbary*, now obsolete), and digging clay (*Right of Marl*, now obsolete) were permitted. Like elsewhere in Britain, commoning was a customary tradition in the New Forest, with rights not formally fixed until the 1854 *Register of Claims to Rights over the Forest*.[93] Commoning rights are linked to property rather than people (and in the cases of Turbary and Marl, to the hearth or chimney), and after 1854 an application had to be made to the Verderers to confirm rights via this Register and gain a commoners brand (a symbol of ownership used to mark ponies and cattle). *Domesday* of 1086, the earliest survey of property in the British Isles, supplies us with many details about

---

93 With thanks to Sylvia Crocker: Netley Marsh History Group

the process of the Norman afforestation of the New Forest, including the associated commoning rights. This has led to the wide assumption that commoning came about as a sort of compensation for the area being turned into a Royal hunting ground; however it is now widely believed that these rights already existed and were simply placed under new restrictions at that time. This point is important for commoners today, who can therefore argue that their rights are ultimately independent of the Crown's interest in the Forest (or any other concern).[94]

Forest Law was different to the common law of the British Isles. As Wise describes, a Royal Forest was a *'kingdom within a kingdom*[95] with its own regulations, byelaws and justice system. Manwood's *Treatise of the Forest Laws* (1598) gives us some idea of the officials that were appointed to enforce Forest Law. The *Riding Forester* and *Woodward* patrolled the New Forest, the *Bowbearer* physically enforced the laws and *Regarders* inspected boundaries and the dogs kept within the Forest. The *Officer of Woods* was responsible for the management of the timber in the Forest (work that became absorbed into the role of the Forestry Commission in 1923).[96] Although the role has evolved over time, another officer of Forest Law was the *Verderer*, a title still in post today. So ancient is the role of Verderer it has even found its way into Forest lore across the British Isles and beyond, specifically the disembodied voices of Verderers believed to still haunt the Forests they patrolled in life.[97]

> *Oyez, Oyez, all manner of persons who have any presentment to make, or matter of things to do at this Court of Verderers, let them come forward and be heard.*

Agisters Call to Court,
Court of Swanimote, Lyndhurst

At one time just Four Verderers held overall responsibility for the enforcement of Forest Law and overseeing hearings in the

---

94 Rose Crespigny & H. Hutchinson: The New Forest – Its Traditions, Inhabitants & Customs
95 The New Forest, its History & its Scenery: JR Wise
96 The Commoners New Forest: FE Kenchington
97 The Forest in Folklore & Mythology: Alexander Porteous

Court of Swanimote & Attachment. Archaically they were rewarded with benefit in kind, being able to hunt any venison they wanted on their way to Court.[98] *The Court of Attachment* was held every 40 days and acted as a preliminary hearing for disputes, transgressions or offences. If the matter could not be resolved at the Court of Attachment (or was considered to be a more serious crime) it would be presented at the higher *Court of Swanimote.* The Court of Swanimote (from the Old English 'swangemot', from *swan* – herdsman and *gemot* - a judicial assembly, also possibly from *Swinemote* - Court of Pannage) was held three times a year, traditionally 15 days before Midsummer, 15 days before the Autumn Equinox and on the 10th November.[99] Some of the punishments for breaking Forest Law were pretty severe, such as the loss of eyes and limbs (including castration!), although their severity lessened over time.[100] Decisions were also made about the general *agistment* (management) of the commoner's stock and other business.

With the removal of the deer in 1851, the role of Verderer changed somewhat. Today, the Verderer exists to represent the commoners, levy dues (such as marking fees and licenses) resolve disputes and enforce byelaws. The number of Verderers has increased to ten; five elected by the commoners (who are required to be landowners with commoning rights) [101] and five others representing various organisations with an interest in the Forest. *Agisters* are employed by the Verderers to assist in the management (*agistment*) and welfare of the commoners' stock. Today, there are five paid *Agisters,* each with a particular part of the Forest to oversee; Kenchington writes that not so long ago there also existed voluntary Agisters, who had arrangements with the local commoners to patrol the Forest and keep an eye on their stock.[102] For anyone interested in the life of an Agister in the early

---

98 Rose Crespigny & H. Hutchinson: The New Forest – Its Traditions, Inhabitants & Customs
99 Manwood's Treatise of the Forest Laws (1598): John Manwood
100 Blood Sport - Hunting in Britain since 1066: Emma Griffin
101 The Commoners New Forest: FE Kenchington
102 The Commoners New Forest: FE Kenchington

1900's, *Jesse Taylor's Diary 1907-1923* is the diary of an agister who recorded his days on the Forest which can be examined at the Christopher Tower Library in Lyndhurst. The Courts of Swanimote & Attachment are now merged into one and otherwise known as the *Verderers Court*, which is held ten times a year at the Verderers Hall in Lyndhurst. This building is believed to stand on the same site of the original ancient Court building that was built in the 1300s and it is possible that the witness box inside the Verderers Court also dates back to the original building, although its official age is currently unknown[103].

The New Forest was designated a National Park in 2005. Although this brought about a protected status, the New Forest is ultimately a working landscape, and there is a worry that the status of 'park' may have contributed to the New Forest being presented more than ever as a tourist attraction. Although visitors are welcomed in the Forest and important to its economy, they can also affect the fragile environment by unwittingly breaking Forest byelaws. For instance, visitors feeding ponies might not realise this can make them aggressive, as well as drawing them towards the roads. And in 2019, instances of cattle worrying by dogs caused cows to start showing aggressive behaviour, which resulted in discussions to remove calves from the Forest and dehorn the cattle. The fact is that without commoning, the landscape would crumble; the opportunity to common is a benefit to local people but also contributes substantially to the ecosystem, a habitat for many plants and animals that would simply not exist here without the stock that roams the Forest.

COLLPIXIE: THE NEW FOREST PONY

The New Forest Pony is perhaps one of the most iconic symbols of the New Forest and is fundamental to the Forest's history, folklore and traditions, having lived indigenous to the New Forest area for over 500,000 years.[104] Contrary to misconception, the ponies on the Forest are not wild; they are all

---

103 You can read more here www.verderers.org.uk.
104 Dionis McNair: New Forest Ponies

owned by local people who *depasture* (turn out) the ponies as part of the ancient tradition of Commoning. The ponies are just one of the five animals that share ancient rights to run on the Forest, the others being cattle, sheep, donkeys and pigs - and they have been kept in this way for many hundreds of years.

The New Forest Pony is hardy and sure-footed, built for the terrain it has evolved in. They have the ability to drop off (lose condition) over the winter, surviving on the lean pickings of Ytene and returning to full condition by late spring. They are happy browsing on furze-tops (gorse) thorn, holme (holly) reeds and forest grasses and hedgerow scrub. The ponies are often described as the architects of the Forest, although in truth, they play this role hand-in-hand with the other animals which roam here. The value of the furze to the New Forest pony was known to be beneficial even for ponies kept in paddocks. The author Irene Soper writes how a pony dealer known as Gypsy Peters collected gorse from the Forest in the hard weather and pounded it with a mallet to make up a forage for his ponies.[105] They also enjoy nettles when the weather turns in the autumn, and you can tell winter is coming because the ponies' tongues turn black from eating them! It is also clear that the New Forest Pony is an instinctive herbalist and self-prescribes from the herbs, wild plants and mineral-rich natural springs found throughout the Forest. Juliette de Bairaci Levy writes how lactating mares *'show much desire for the tiny flowering shoots of the white and blue milkwort which is abundant... this small plant increases milk production.'* The ponies will also seek out *sticky-willy* (cleavers), which is considered a tonic for the blood, and also wild garlic, which acts as a natural wormer. My pony is very keen to get hold of these wayside plants at any cost (usually mine, as I am dragged through a hedge or into a muddy ditch).

The earliest depiction of the New Forest Pony is of a pack-pony, found on a pot in the north-west of the New Forest in Linwood, dating around 300AD.[106] The ancestor of the New

---

105 Irene Soper: The Romany Way
106 Dionis McNair: New Forest Ponies

Forest Pony would have been small, around 12 hands (many stand to around 14 hands today) with a shaggy coat, beard and moustache. In an effort to 'improve' the breed, in the 1700 & 1800's a number of stallions from livelier breeds were introduced into the Forest such as Thoroughbreds, Arabs and Spanish horses. Some of the New Forest bloodlines then became bigger and finer. However, they also lost some of their hardiness and individuality and the New Forest Pony was in danger of extinction. Thanks to the efforts of early breeding enthusiasts however, the breed has endured and bred back to be truer to 'type'.

Today, the ponies are perfectly designed to negotiate the often boggy and uneven terrain of the New Forest and often (although not always!) have an innate knowing of what ground to avoid, showing this skill at its best during the annual New Forest Point-to-Point pony races. As a local saying would have it, the ponies negotiate the terrain 'like a flea in the grass' where other breeds may falter. They are also hardy animals - although some ponies are stud-bred, others have spent most of their lives living out on the Forest, usually not far from their owners' smallholding. They used to be called home with the pony-call *'kip, kip!'* which summons the 'work-a-day' ponies.[107] One local friend of mine remembers his grandfather keeping ponies in this way. On needing to cross the Forest he would walk out onto the heath and find one of his ponies, which were usually nearby (muddy and probably wild as the hills), sling a rope halter on, and ride off! The capability of the New Forest Pony to endure and traverse the environment seems both ancestral and intuitive; an inherent ability to navigate the safest ways across the moors and the darkest parts of the New Forest. Interestingly, these dark places were locally referred to as *hell* [108] from *helan* 'to cover' (such as *Helclose* and *Hellcorner*, both mentioned within the 1670 perambulation) but perhaps also suggests how unpredictable the Forest can be even to those who know it intimately.

---

107 Heywood Sumner: The New Forest
108 John Richard de Capel Wise: The New Forest, Its History & Its Scenery

When the flies are at their worst, the forest-run New Forest Pony often congregates in places on the Forest known as '*shades*'. These are breezy greens or spots on higher ground where the flies are less of a nuisance, such as *Latchmore Shade* near Ogdens. There are hundreds of these shades in the New Forest, which have been used by Forest stock for thousands of years. Many were named and marked on some of the earliest maps of the Forest, although very few are remembered on modern OS maps. Here, the ponies huddle together with their heads turned inward to protect from the flies and other irritating insects, the ponies and cattle being described as 'all in a shade'. Incidentally, the Forest is generally out of bounds to horses from outside the area during the summer because of the New Forest Crabfly, otherwise known locally as the *Stoat*. Forest-bred ponies have built up a tolerance to these pests, but other horses cannot bear them, and it can be quite dangerous to ride in the summer months unless your horse has been born and bred in the Forest.

Superstition & Folklore

The horse has long been associated with old customs, magic and witchcraft across the British Isles and Northern Europe, so it is not surprising that the same applies in the New Forest where the pony has endured as an important part of local ethos and economy. In the Hampshire and Dorset region there was a whole host of folk superstition surrounding the horse, from high-held mares' tails forecasting bad weather to more complicated folk charms. Knotted horsehair was used for fertility or to cure goitre[109] as well as plaiting into rings which were considered to have lucky powers (particularly horsehair from piebald or skewbald ponies). Another custom was the hanging of blacksmith *churms* (charms)[110] or hag stones (holed stones) by the stable doors for protection or above the horse, hung from the rafters in the centre of the stable.[111] In the north of England, the hag stone is known as a dobbie stone from *dubh* (black) referring to the *Dobbie*,

---

109 Janet Farrar & Virginia Russell: The Magical History of the Horse
110 Frederick Robins: The Smith
111 The Pattern Under The Plough: George Ewart Evans

a spectral black horse seen through a hag stone or in the periphery vision. Whilst conjecture, it's likely that a similar belief was held about hag stones and the local New Forest fairy the *Collepixie.*

Another custom in Hampshire involved mounting the hooves from a dead horse above a stable door to protect its orphaned foal to ensure it inherited the good qualities of the mare[112] (probably her feet – the old proverb, 'no foot, no horse' comes to mind here). Many similar customs still survive in the New Forest today, in particular the fear of your depastured pony being *elvish-marked*[113] with plaits and hag-ridden by malicious spirits. Indeed, the Forest can appear a mysterious landscape to those who cross the grids. The ponies have a knowledge of this often-treacherous playground, avoiding a fate at the hands of the dreaded *Collepixie.*

The Collepixie or Colt Pixy

The Collepixie is a local trickster spirit that takes the shape of a New Forest Pony and entices walkers, horses and their riders into the treacherous bogs of the New Forest; according to local lore, only the eldest-born sibling is protected from his spell.[114] The spirit is usually described as small 'wild' looking pony with a long and rough pale coat, or a sleek and handsome young colt (a young male pony) or sometimes *'a beautiful filly* (female) *lightly stepping, with waving mane and tail'*[115] which lures the unwitting traveller to their untimely demise. The Colt-Pixy is also associated with the hag-riding of horses; ponies who were found in the morning sweated-up and/or with rough wind-plaits in their mane, were believed to have been charmed by the Colt Pixy into a wild gallop throughout the night. The local term *'as ragged as a Colt Pixy'* refers to a person or animal who looks as wild and untamed as the Colt-Pixy itself - or as an exhausted pony that had been led upon a wild hag-ride. The Puck or Colt Pixy is also known to claim harvest

112 Janet Farrar & Virginia Russell: The Magical History of the Horse
113 Shakespeare's Richard III
114 John Richard de Capel Wise: The New Forest, Its History & Its Scenery
115 Wanderers in the New Forest, Juliette de Bairacli Levy

offerings at the festival of Samhain, which marks the end of the farming year.

> *I am that merry wanderer of the night*
> *When I, a fat and bean-fed horse beguile*
> *Neighing in likeness of a filly foal.*

Shakespeare: A Midsummer Nights Dream

The Pixy name is often used interchangeably in the Forest with that of the mischievous spirit Puck - *Pukah/Pwca/Pooka/Phooka, Hob* or the Cornish *Bucca, Horse-Hag* or *Fairy Hob*[116], all 'devil' names used interchangeably for the ancient chthonic land gods and spirits of place, who, according to some, were diminished demi-gods or piskies.[117] From the Old English *deofol*, from the 1200's the word referred to a *'subordinate evil spirit afflicting humans; false god, heathen god.'* The author Thomas Crocker relays from an Irish boy in 1825,

> *'the Phookas were very numerous in times long ago; they*
> *were wicked-minded, black-looking bad things, that would*
> *come in the form of wild colts (horses) with chains hanging*
> *about them … The Phookas did great hurt to benighted*
> *travellers.'*[118]

The earliest surviving written account of the Colt Pixy or Collepixie dates back to around the 1500's from a play, *'I shall be ready at thine elbow to play the part of the hobgoblin or Collepixie*'[119]. In 1627 more details are given on the treacherous nature of the spirit-horse: *'...still walking light a ragged-colt, often out of a bush does bolt, of purpose to deceive us, and leading us makes us to stray...and when we stick in mire or clay, Hob doth with laughter leave us.'*

The Colt-Pixy's impression upon the local place names and superstitions suggests it has very early origins in the New Forest. Many places in the New Forest are named after this spirit, in some instances indicating dangerous patches of ground or otherwise places known to be haunted by the spirit. Plenty of places in the

---

116 John Richard de Capel Wise: The New Forest, Its History & Its Scenery
117 Traditional Witchcraft, A Cornish Book of Ways: Gemma Gary
118 Fairy Legends & Traditions of the South of Ireland: Thomas C Croker
119 The Apophthegmes of Erasmus, 1531

New Forest include these names such as Pixey Field, Pucks Hill (near Puckpits inclosure) Pixy Mead and Pucksmoor, amongst others.

> *But when ye have killed, and your bowl is spilled,*
> *And your shoes are clean outworn,*
> *Back ye must speed for all that ye need,*
> *To oak, and ash, and thorn!*

A Tree Song, Puck of Pook's Hill,
Rudyard Kipling

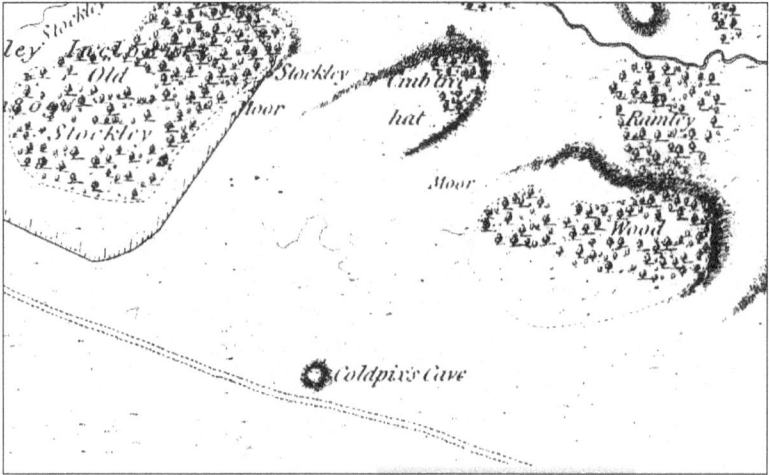

COLD PIX'S CAVE (BARROW) 1789 DRIVERS MAP

One particular site in the Forest is especially concerned with the story of the Colt-Pixy. Near Beaulieu aerodrome there stands a round barrow known as the *Cold Pix's Cave* which, when partially excavated in the 1940's, was found to contain an amber necklace. This tumulus is known locally to be a haunt of the Colt Pixy, and several riders have had experiences with their horses being spooked near this round barrow (including my own stubborn pony, who made it quite clear to me that he 'would-not-will-not' pass this particular spot, well before I knew anything of its history). Barrows in the Forest were sometimes also believed to be the mass burial sites of commoners' ponies[120] although there is no truth in this.

The Colt Pixy is not the only changeling horse-spirit from folklore to be credited with enchanting men and animals to their watery demise. One similar spirit is the *Kelpie* - a word which itself may be derived from the word 'Colt' - which usually appears as a grey or black pony with hooves pointing backwards and who can change shape at will. The Kelpie also has a reputation for luring travellers or livestock into the water by singing or whinnying, before dragging them under and devouring them. If a Kelpie mates with a normal horse, it is said that the offspring will always lie down and roll in water with their rider when crossing a river or ford. Other places in the New Forest are known to have ominous watery connotations, such as Latchmoor *'the pond of corpses*'[121] , and perhaps we might encounter the Pixy-Colt on the shore, such as at Tanners Lane in Lymington where the ponies are still able to wander onto the beach.

Traditions & Trades

In the past the horse was a central part of everyday life and it was possible to make a living by breeding and trading ponies. Modern living has meant that the demand for ponies is much reduced and making a living from the ponies alone is unrealistic, yet many commoners still continue for tradition's sake and their love of the breed. They are offered a subsidy as part of the Grazing Scheme for turning out their ponies as they are vital to the ecology of the Forest. Funding is also offered to the owners of the stallions, a small number of quality purebred animals that do not roam the Forest all year round but are released across the New Forest from late spring onwards to cover the mares and ensure new generations of the breed. This youngstock can be taken off the Forest in later years, if the owner wishes, during *drifts* and *colthunting,* and money can still be made by selling foals with a

---

120 Hugh Pasmore: A New Forest Commoner Remembers
121 Horace Hutchinson: The New Forest

quality bloodline or breaking (training) ponies for riding and showing. In these cases, they can become incredibly valuable.

Between August and November, the ponies are rounded up by the Agisters and their owners on horseback during 15 or more drifts. During these drifts, which have been held since medieval times, the ponies are driven across the Forest by a team of local riders who use natural obstacles to channel the Forest ponies in certain directions and into pounds (holding pens) for inspection and routine procedures. Each owner has a unique symbol of ownership which is crafted into a brand, and the drifts can be an opportunity to carry out ownership branding on young ponies, a practice which is momentarily uncomfortable for the pony but ensures its ownership (and therefore care) is secured. These branding irons often hold a special superstition in the hearts of those living in the cottages where the brand was originally registered, often being kept above the fireplace in memory of the properties' commoning rights and branded onto cottage or stable doors.[122] Tail marking (trimming tail hair to different patterns, known locally as *terraces* or *flounces*) is also carried out during drifts, to indicate the designated Agister in charge of the particular area of the Forest the pony is run on. Indeed the Crown referred to the Agisters as *marksmen*, derived from their function of marking the horses and cattle.[123] This is helpful in quickly identifying where a stray animal is supposed to be. Whilst the ponies generally stay within their haunts – a radius of about 2 or 3 miles – they are sometimes known to stray out of their usual patch.

Colthunting is a similar event which takes place when certain ponies have been identified either for breaking as riding ponies or to be sold. Once spotted on the Forest by the Colthunters, the pony may be driven into a pound but sometimes caught on the move by riders with rope, who then bring the pony to a standstill by pulling up their own horses.[124] The pounds played an equally

122 Hugh Pasmore: A Commoner Remembers
123 Rose Crespigny & H. Hutchinson: The New Forest – Its Traditions, Inhabitants & Customs
124 Hugh Pasmore: A Commoner Remembers

important role in the impoundment of wayward ponies who roamed outside the Forest boundaries (locally referred to as *'lane creepers'*) before the Forest was fenced and cattlegrids been installed in 1962. Ponies that strayed outside the boundaries were either rounded up by landowners who then charged a fee to release them to the owner, or, if not yet branded, at risk of being claimed by someone else.

EXAMPLES OF COMMONERS BRAND MARKS, NEW FOREST MERITAGE MUSEUM

Ponies identified for sale are taken to local stock sales, such as the famous Beaulieu Road sale, which continues to trade in the archaic currency of Guineas. The sales were popular with local people, but also people from outside of the Forest who would travel long distances to bid. The Romanies were also fond of buying, breaking and trading Forest ponies, which they described as *'black gold whinnying in the hedgerows'*.

An industry integral to the towns and villages of the New Forest was the blacksmith and farrier, who shod both working and riding horses in the Forest (as well as the occasional cow!) The blacksmith has always been considered as a magical trade and this would almost certainly have been the case in the New Forest where charcoal was so plentiful and old traditions, particularly those related to horsemanship, were held in such high regard. Indeed, just like the New Forest traditions of commoning and charcoal burning, the trade of the Blacksmith was usually a family craft, handed down from generation to generation. The Blacksmiths' Forge was a common sight in New Forest villages and towns right up to the 1950's, vital to so many people whose livelihoods relied upon horsepower or the shaping of metal in one way or another. The Blacksmith also carried out the ringing of pigs on the Forest, a practice which continues today, allowing pigs to forage free-range on the Forest (called Pannage, or the Right of Mast) without destroying the ground by uprooting the earth. They were also believed to have healing gifts, such as the ability to stop the flow of blood and cure all things with the water from their troughs.[125] One Blacksmith, operating in the 1600's, was referred to as *'an excellent farrier, who shall ever-be furnished with horseshoes, nayles and drugges, both for inward and outward applications'.*[126] As such, the Blacksmith even played the part of the village vet, inventing their own clinical equipment such as the Balling Iron and the Popgun (designed to dispense balls of herbs and medicine to the back of the throat of cattle and horses). Another practice was retrieving the milt (a small oval-shaped mass looking like a

---

125 Janet Farrar & Virginia Russell: The Magical History of the Horse
126 Frederick Robins: The Smith

spleen, sometimes found in a foal's mouth at birth) which, when combined with various oils and other processes, could be used to charm horses. Sybil Leek gives details on how a similar process was used by a New Forest Romany: he sold a horse to a *Gorgio* (non-Gypsy), then used the charm to cause the pony to escape and return to him time and time again, until the owner sold it back to the Romany for half the price he bought it.[127]

18TH C. BLACKSMITH CHARM; ILLUSTRATION FROM F. ROBINS, THE SMITH

Iron horseshoes and nails were used as simple charms to protect the home, whilst blacksmiths made more sophisticated amulets out of iron to protect against the evil eye.[128] Horse brasses with symbols such as the sun, greenery, hobgoblins and lucky horseshoes were also made to protect horses as they worked. The moon was a particularly frequent symbol to decorate horse trappings, being associated with various aspects of horsemanship including shoeing: *'continue the shooing of him ... until his heels be well shaped and large which will be infallibly after twice or thrice shooing; do it at the change, about the forth or fifth day of the new moon.*[129] Another device used on a horse and carriage was the rumble bell, a round metal

---

127 Sybil Leek: Diary of a Witch
128 Janet Farrar & Virginia Russell: The Magical History of the Horse
129 The Compleat Horseman, 1711

bell with a loud jingle that warned pedestrians of an approaching horse-drawn vehicle; complete examples are rare, but a few have been found in and around the New Forest.

The association between horses, mischievous faeries and protection against them was clearly an ongoing concern for the people of Hampshire. A Forge once stood in Pokesdown (previously Pucks Down), a town just outside the New Forest which was once a heath covered in iron age barrows. Local lore says that around the Forge was planted a number of horse chestnut trees.[130] There is mixed folklore about horse chestnuts. Some say that the conkers were ground up and fed to horses to relieve coughs - however horse chestnuts can cause toxicity in horses, so this is unlikely. Perhaps this was in fact the sweet chestnut, which is safe to eat, or maybe the trees were planted due to their reputation for warding off unwanted visitors (in this case the Pixy Colt) who were repelled by the toxic chestnut. Of course, the chestnut trees with their broad leaves may also have offered shade for the horses waiting to be shod.

> It once was known as "Puck's Down" in the happy long ago,
> Which suggests a scene of fairyland, with romance all aglow ...
> ... I call to mind the Pokesdown Wood; in memory I see
> Its grace and charm, which some while back brought happiness to me.

Cumberland Clark:
The Bournemouth Song Book

One of the most fabled of the New Forest forges was the forge opposite the New Queen Pub in Avon, just outside of Ringwood, where it is said Sir Walter Tirel had his horses' shoes reversed after fleeing the scene of the murder of William II or William 'Rufus' ('Red') in 1100. As late as the 19th century, the blacksmith's forge at Avon had to pay an annual fine of three pounds and 10 shillings as penalty for this treachery.[131] Another forge in Lynes Lane was demolished and turned into housing in the 1930's; however it is said that the blacksmiths anvil (which

130 Frederick Robins: The Smith
131 The Folklore of Hampshire and the Isle of Wight: Wendy Boase

was too heavy to move from the site) is buried under the bungalow's back doorstep. Indeed, the Blacksmith's anvil is a powerful charm in itself, and it was known that a Blacksmith (or descendants of a Blacksmith) could curse on an anvil by turning it upside down and/or turning it anti-clockwise while chanting malicious words.[132]

> *Sir Walter Tyrrell, years ago, according to tradition,*
> *Crossed the Avon at this spot and tried a new position ...*
> *He had his horse shod the wrong way round, his hurried*
> *tracks to smother;*
> *So when he started one way, his pursuers went the other.*
>
> Cumberland Clark, The Bournemouth Song Book

Nowadays the New Forest forges have been converted into houses, pubs and garages, but immortalised in many local road and house names such as Smithy Lane, Blacksmith Cottage and Old Smithy. Some of the most iconic New Forest forges, however, had a somewhat 'semi-permanent' appearance and were made with straw roofs. One such straw forge stood at Gorley Green; luckily for us, it was immortalised by an artist named Beale in the 1800's.

BLACKSMITH'S SHOP AT GORLEY GREEN: ILLUSTRATION BY BEALE, 1885

---

132 Janet Farrar & Virginia Russell: The Magical History of the Horse

The New Forest Pony is popular with visitors to the New Forest, who enjoy watching herds sleeping in the sunshine or having a *ronge* (a local term for horseplay). Their popularity does however bring problems, as visitors touch and (worse) feed the ponies, unwittingly leading to ponies being drawn to roads where they may be killed, falling sick due to eating unsuitable food, and behaving aggressively. Unless you want to find yourself between two semi-feral animals weighing half a tonne each, duelling over a carrot, then please enjoy the ponies from a distance!

THE HAMPSHIRE HOG: THE COMMON OF MAST

Pannage or *Common of Mast* is a right held by a number of properties within the Forest, allowing pigs to be turned out as part of the ancient tradition of commoning. The pigs are allowed to roam the Forest during a period not less than 56 days (mid-September to mid-November as fixed by the Forestry Commission and Verderers), although the period is sometimes extended if the acorn crop is particularly heavy. During Pannage the pigs enjoy *Mast* or *Ovest* - the first flush of forest tree fruits such as acorns, beechnuts and chestnuts that carpet the autumnal Forest floor. Perfectly designed for foraging, the pigs roam loose in the Forest and enjoy rummaging through the leaf litter and surface soil for the tasty autumnal fruits (known locally as *rootling*). This is by far one of my favourite events of year. The pigs have open access to my driveway and around the outside of our cottage, where they spend a considerable amount of time trying to wreck the lawn and keeping me awake at night with their snorting and squeaking. They seem to like pulling all-nighters and only start to think about sleep just before dawn. When they do settle, they usually sleep into the mid-morning, like teenagers. They like to curl up together, normally in my parking space and spread themselves out when I drive away.

PIGS IN MY PARKING SPACE

All pigs are nose-ringed, a procedure which in earlier times was often carried out by the blacksmith but is today performed by a vet. Nose-ringing is only momentarily uncomfortable for the pigs and ensures their continued freedom on the Forest to forage through vegetation and leaf litter without causing too much destruction to fence lines or fragile ecosystems by digging too deeply. All pigs turned out on the Forest are required to have at least three rings.

History of Pigs in the New Forest

Domesticated around 7000 BCE, pigs are an integral part of rural history. The New Forest is certainly no exception and in fact quite unique, with swine continuing to be kept in a manner that has remained largely unchanged for thousands of years. As such the pig and its ancestor, the Wild Boar (which was historically classed as one of the ancient wild beasts or 'Deor' of the New Forest), are embedded in local tradition and folklore. In fact, the New Forest was one of the last strongholds of the Wild Boar before its eradication; Anthony Dent tells us in his fabulous *Lost Beasts of Britain* that the last recorded Wild Boar to be killed in the British Isles was shot by a keeper in the New Forest in the late 1800's. A vague piece of local lore says that an inkstand was made of its trotter, which was kept at the Verderers Court. Whilst it may be true that the inkstand once existed, I have spoken to a long-standing member of staff from the Verderers Court who says she has never heard of it. If it did once exist, it is certainly not at the Court today.[133] Another story relating to boars in the Forest comes from a 1913 newspaper cutting that describes how two boars were presented by the King to Lord Montagu, but which escaped from their enclosure. One was soon found, the other surviving roaming wild in the New Forest for 18 months! It was eventually found in Denny Wood, where it was shot dead.[134]

Many of our New Forest ancestors lived on modest incomes, with many poorer families only managing to gain property by obtaining peppercorn smallholder tenancies or through the folk custom of the *one-night-house* (essentially, a form of squatting). Pigs were easy to breed and could be fed on scraps and the roughage of the Forest and were an essential part of the livelihood of New Forest families. Pork would generally have been the staple meat on the table, usually having come from an animal they reared themselves and Hampshire would become known for its quality pork and bacon. Penny Legg writes[135] that Hampshire people were affectionately known as 'Hampshire Hogs', a term derived from the fine pigs and bacon produced in the county - in 1790 it could be found in the dictionary as a *'jocular appellation for a Hampshire man'* that is, a term of endearment. The writer Charlotte Yonge of Hursley writes in *'An Old Woman's Outlook'* (1892), *'I do not know whether the Hampshire man is more devoted to his pig than the natives of other counties, but it certainly fills an important place in the family possessions … scarcely a house is without a tidy pigsty.'* Many of the old cottages in the Forest had ancient pigsties with hatches for turning pigs out into the woods during Pannage season, and several of these ancient sties still exist today, although most are no longer used for their original purpose.[136]

---

133 With thanks to the Verderers Court, Lyndhurst
134 Hampshire Independent, March 1913
135 Folklore of Hampshire: Penny Legg
136 Verderers of the New Forest: A. Pasmore

Perfectly adapted for survival, the original New Forest pig was known for its wild and rugged appearance. They were black, bristly and stout animals, very unlike the domestic pigs in other areas of the UK. Illustrations of New Forest pigs published in such works as William Gilpin's *Remarks on Forest Scenery* of 1786 depict these hairy, hardy animals with short, rounded backs and pricked ears, much like the wild boar in appearance. Rose Crespigny writes in 1899 how, *'one of the most frequent sights of the Forest, in the autumn, is an old black sow followed by her troop of lesser, but equally black, offspring.*[137] Excavations show that ancient Hampshire pigs were *'taller at the shoulder but shorter in the back ... and retained many of the Wild Boar characteristics'.*[138] The wild boar survived in the New Forest right up until the 1800's. Given the unparalleled freedom of domestic sows during the Autumn, male boars would have had plenty of opportunity to breed with them and introduce wild boar characteristics to domestic New Forest pigs - such as the Wessex Saddleback, a breed that originates from the New Forest area known locally as the *Shaded Pig*[139] (now listed as a rare breed) and the sandy-coloured *'badger-pied'* pig.[140] However, old traditions die hard in the Forest, and we are still lucky to see large numbers of dark, bristly pigs rootling around in the undergrowth during Pannage.

Several places in the Forest are named in memory of swine and their husbandry, such as Everton *'the wild-boar place'*[141] and their connection with the rural economy cannot be understated. Pigs were even used to value land; in *Domesday* (1086) we find woodlands being valued by the number of pigs they could maintain; for instance statements such as *'silva de 20 porcis'* meaning a woodland capable of supporting twenty pigs.[142]

---

137 Rose Crespigny & H. Hutchinson: The New Forest – Its Traditions, Inhabitants & Customs
138 Heywood Sumner: A Winter Walk in the New Forest
139 Rose Crespigny & H. Hutchinson: The New Forest – Its Traditions, Inhabitants & Customs
140 John Richard de Capel Wise: The New Forest, Its History & Its Scenery
141 John Richard de Capel Wise: The New Forest, Its History & Its Scenery
142 John Richard de Capel Wise: The New Forest, Its History & Its Scenery

The Fairy Ring Pound in Pinnick - restored & explained.

ILLUSTRATION FROM HEYWOOD SUMNER; A WINTER WALK IN THE NEW FOREST

The Common of Mast

The term Mast (or *Akermast* collectively) originates from the Old English for *'fallen nuts, food for swine/ to fatten, feed'* and Ovest from the Old English for *'fruit produce'*. Although the word 'Pannage' is most often used to describe the tradition, the origin of this word in particular is connected with the fee paid by the owners to retain the right. The word was used interchangeably in Middle English with *Pawnnage,* describing not only the act or right of pasturing swine in woods but also the monetary charge.[143] In Wessex the title of *Hogward* was given to the Guardian of Pannage payments, as recorded in the nearby Forest of Bere. During the passage of time, the title became distorted into the surname, 'Howard'.

The pigs certainly enjoy foraging for natural food and have an unparalleled amount of freedom during the Pannage season, but they are home-loving animals. Unlike the New Forest Ponies, who often rest wherever they roam, the New Forest pigs will often choose to return home at dusk for their home comforts. Writing in the late 1700s, the author William Gilpin tells us how a drove of Forest pigs were taught to return home for their dinner each night by sounding a horn, and *'...(the keeper) then turns them*

---

143 H. Hutchinson: The New Forest

into the litter (bracken bed) *where, after a long journey, and a hearty meal, they sleep deliciously.*'[144] Incidentally, the use of bracken as animal bedding is a tradition still practiced in some parts of the Forest today. In autumn, bracken from the open Forest is cut and baled, usually into large round bales, traditionally after Michaelmas Day. Another role the pigs historically played in the Forest was seeking out the truffle, an underground fungus hunted by its scent.

The beginning of the Pannage season can cause some apprehension in horse riders on the New Forest, as horses who have not seen a pig for some 12 months get the scent of them on the air. There is an old saying, *'to horses pigs smell like death'*. This association is possibly an ancestral memory in the horse from previous generations being ridden in wild boar hunts. The Wild Boar, or Old English 'Eofor' was depicted on battle helmets throughout the Middle Ages, an instrument of war seen akin to the nature and build of this creature and, as so common with hunting myth and magic, assimilated the hunter with his prey. With broad chests and sharp tusks, it was renowned for charging underneath the horse and goring the stomach open: *'When he seeth unavoidable death, he singleth out one of the huntsmen and will run upon him with the greatest rage imaginable.'*[145] The boar was hunted to the point of extinction before more were introduced from the Continent – although the introduced boars often proved more aggressive than their predecessors and became *'terrible to travellers'*.[146] To be attacked by a wild boar would often prove fatal, although Barbara de Seyssel, a local woman from the New Forest, gives a New Forest rhyme[147] which describes a traditional cure:

> *'If thou art hurt by a Hart (stag) t'will bring thee to thy bier.*
> *But a swab of tar will a Boar's hurt heal, of that have thou no*
> *fear.'*

---

144 William Gilpin: Remarks on Forest Scenery
145 Nicolas Cox: The Gentleman's Recreation
146 John Aubrey: The Natural History of Wiltshire
147 Anthony Dent: Lost Beasts of Britain

Barbara was a fascinating woman who lived in a caravan in Lyndhurst before moving to the secluded Holmhill Cottage in the woods near Burley. She came to the New Forest on 'pony patrol', a job which involved preventing the ponies from straying out of the Forest boundaries before the cattle grids were installed in the 1960's. The author Anthony Pasmore, who knew her personally, describes her as an *'accomplished horsewoman, amateur archaeologist, expert on woodland crafts, hunter, and traveller'.*[148] Pasmore continues that Holmhill Cottage was demolished after Barbara's death in 1977 and, *'if any part of the New Forest is haunted, it is for me those silent and still relatively undisturbed woods of Holmhill.'*

The Common of Mast also plays an important part in the wider ecological balance of the Forest. Whilst pigs can safely enjoy the first flush of green acorns, they can prove lethal to cattle and ponies as they contain toxic tannins, which in excess can cause damage to the liver and kidneys. The release of hundreds of eager little pigs at the first flush of Autumn ensures the number of acorns is controlled. Charlotte Yonge writes that when *'combined with the other delicacies of the season* (the pigs) *do themselves no harm'.*[149] In a so-called *Mast Year* when exceptional numbers of

148 Anthony Pasmore: New Forest Notes (Lymington Times September 1994)
149 Charlotte Yonge: An Old Womans Outlook in a Hampshire Village

nuts are produced (for the oak tree, usually about every 7 years) pigs may be released earlier or the season extended. Once the acorns have turned from green to brown, they are safe for other animals to eat and the pigs are removed from the Forest.

Whilst it may seem tempting to allow all pigs to remain out, this can cause a shortage of food supplies for the animals who are over-wintered on the Forest – even the deer, for whom brown acorns are an important winter foodstuff. Pigs have also been known to break through into people's gardens and winter crops when the acorn supplies start to run low, which can cause disputes – although, in the Forest the responsibility lies with the homeowner to ensure their fencing is stock-proof. There is a saying on the Forest, *"Good fences make good neighbours"*! There are some exceptions to the rule, however. Some breeding sows, locally called *Queen Sows* or *Sows of Privilege* are allowed to remain on the Forest beyond the Pannage season, providing they are well behaved and always return home at sunset.

Pigs & the Underworld

The association of pigs and death is also one concerned with the agricultural affairs of the season; with the old festival of Samhain (pronounced *sow-in*, 1st November) marking the beginning of a period of slaughter after the pigs are taken off the Forest for smoking or salting. In Hampshire, it was traditional to cut the meat into joints and smoke it over the fire in the chimney.[150] Pork was an essential supply for winter stores for our ancestors and is still popular in the Forest today, where Pannage sausages and pork can be found for sale in local farm shops. Samhain also marks the completion of the fruit harvests, with preserves being made and stored for winter. In Hampshire, the saying goes that any crops not harvested before 31st October will be ruined by the faeries who start weeing on the blackberries![151] It is common in the Forest to see seasonal fruits and meats prepared together, such as pork and apple sausages. The meat is

---

150 Charlotte Yonge: An Old Womans Outlook in a Hampshire Village
151 Vikki Bramshaw: Craft of the Wise

local, free-range, fed on natural food, contributes towards the balance of the Forest ecology and supports the local economy. The pig or boar has also found itself part of the New Forest expression to *'rattle like a boar in a holme* (holly) *bush'*, meaning to excessively talk[152] i.e. rattle on.

Returning to the Old English word for Boar, *Eofor*, we find a connection with the Hampshire Hog, witchcraft and the underworld. The *Eofor-Spreot*, a barbed spear used for hunting boar, was the weapon used by the hero in the Old English epic Beowulf to fight the underwater witch, *Grendel's Mother*. The spear was in fact her own, found by Boewulf in her cave. In Wales, the goddess Cerridwyn is referred to as *The White Sow* and had the power to assume the shape of a pig. And the Greek witch-goddess Circe had the power to turn men into swine (and did so frequently!) We also find in records of various witch trials that the form of a pig was a favourite for shapeshifting witches, and even for the devil himself.[153] Whilst we do not know that pigs were considered in a similar way in Wessex, this was often the case and whilst only being conjecture, probably very likely in the Forest, a place so anciently connected with the pig. Across the British Isles, pigs were also known to predict the weather: gusty weather was indicated by pigs tossing straw around their pen or otherwise (for the unluckier pig) by examining the fat on its spleen.

History has shown that mankind has also shared an enjoyment of acorns with the pig. Acorn coffee was popular in the New Forest and beyond during WW1 and WW2 when it was not possible to import coffee beans, whilst the ancient Britons of Hampshire were known to feed babies on a mixture of crushed acorns and milk.[154] Hugh Pasmore recalls a New Forest expression, *'Babies is like pigs. So long as you give them full bellies and dry beds, they be happy.'*[155]

---

152 John Richard de Capel Wise: The New Forest, Its History & Its Scenery
153 Raven Grimassi: Encyclopaedia of Wicca & Witchcraft
154 Charlotte Yonge: An Old Woman's Outlook in a Hampshire Village
155 Hugh Pasmore: A New Forest Commoner Remembers

FOREST-RUN CATTLE

'The wholesome, spicy-sweet, drowsy smell of cow.'[156]

Whilst the pony is probably considered the most iconic animal of the New Forest, in terms of the Forest's complete history, ecology and economy, the cattle are equally important. The auroch, ancient ancestor of the domestic cow, roamed this part of the country from the latter end of the Ice Age. The auroch was a much larger and broader animal than our modern cow, approximately a third larger than a large-breed bull, and with proportionally longer legs. It also had huge, curved horns - and to support them, a thick and wide skull. It was an important animal to our ancestors, depicted in cave art, hunted as a source of food and eventually domesticated. By the Neolithic period domestic cattle had been selectively bred into existence although the auroch would not become extinct until the start of the Bronze Age.

Cattle have been kept on the Forest for thousands of years for both milk, beef and as draft ox, described in the history books as *'beasts of the plough'*;[157] the word *bugle* was used here and elsewhere to describe the ox. Cattle were also used as currency, or barter, as early as 9000 BCE. The word 'cattle' comes from the Anglo-Norman *catel*, for a sum of money and the Old English *feoh* for property and shares its root origins with the word 'capital' and also with 'kin', possibly suggesting the symbiotic relationship that man once had with his cattle.[158]

In the New Forest, cattle were important to the local landscape for controlling the scrub. They remain so today, as one of three 'architects' of the Forest. As the old Forest saying goes, *'the deer started the work, the ponies followed it up, and the cattle finished it'*.[159] Although there have been some recent disputes about overgrazing, most agree the pros outweigh the cons. A drop in the number of stock or deer on the Forest can cause dramatic

---

156 The Commoners New Forest: FE Kenchington
157 The Commoners New Forest: FE Kenchington
158 Changeling Cattle & Magical Cows: Patricia Monaghan
159 The Commoners New Forest: FE Kenchington

changes in the landscape, with many of the open lawns starting to be lost to gorse and other scrub. While some people might see this as a 'rewilding', that is far from the truth: it is in fact an influx of fast-growing bullies overcoming more fragile ecosystems. The animals play an important part in retaining a balance, with farmers offered a subsidy as part of the Grazing Scheme for turning out cattle which are vital to the ecology of the Forest.

Unlike the ponies, the New Forest does not have its own specific breed of cattle. However, there was a cross-bred animal which once ran the Forest and could have been close to a traditional Forest breed. The 'Forest Cow' was brindle-coloured, hardy and small-framed, and very efficient at converting the poor grass and forage of the New Forest into milk. Its origins are unknown, but was likely a mixture of Channel Island, Shorthorn, Guernsey and Ayrshire blood. It is also possible that some Normandy blood was introduced. Beaulieu Abbey (which held many farms in the area) had been established as part of the Cistercian Order in Citeaux, France, and it's likely they chose to introduce breeding stock from their own Normandy cattle into the British Forest-run stock.[160] Incidentally, according to local lore, Beaulieu Abbey was founded by King John in 1205 after he believed himself to be cursed by bad dreams, which involved the dead monks who he rode down at Lincoln.[161] It is also believed that the site of Beaulieu Abbey was on (or near) the site of a small chapel that served the once-village of Thorougham - perhaps another attempt by King John to attempt to appease the Almighty for previous wrongs. Today, the cattle roaming the New Forest are mostly crossbreeds including Angus and Hereford blood, with some belted Galloway. Cattle such as the belted Galloway, with its body a different colour to its fore and hind parts, is described here in the New Forest as a *'shadow cow'*.[162] There are also some gorgeous examples of English Longhorn in the north of the Forest. Most of the cattle running on the Forest are bred for beef.

---

160 The Commoners New Forest: FE Kenchington
161 The History of Hunting in Hampshire: Brig. Gen. JFR Hope
162 John Richard de Capel Wise: The New Forest, Its History & Its Scenery

Milk herds do still exist, although they are rare - a reflection of the downfall of the dairy industry nationwide. Writing in 1899 De Crespigny & Hutchinson describe the call to milking, *'coop! coop!'* used by cattle farmers in the New Forest.[163]

There is little folklore surrounding cattle specific to the New Forest, however for comparisons we can look to similar rural communities in the British Isles where legends have been preserved, as it is more than likely that in a community so reliant on its cattle and other stock similar traditions would have persisted. For instance, a wealth of fairy folklore and bedtime stories describe how faeries steal and spoil milk and cream, and in many places in the UK it was considered important to appease them to avoid them affecting milk yields. There are also a number of superstitions surrounding the eating of beef. As folklore would have it, any cow that was suddenly found dead was believed to have been 'stolen' by the faeries and replaced with a dead fairy. It was therefore considered taboo to eat the flesh of the animal, which was quickly buried instead.[164] It was also customary to bury a slipped (aborted) calf in a place where the herd regularly passed (such as a gateway) as a sympathetic charm to prevent other cows in the herd being affected.[165] Another piece of folklore describes how a red thread should be tied to a heifers' tail to dissuade the faeries and protect it from bewitchment, otherwise its calf might die during the calving.[166] Once born, the afterbirth should be thrown into a thorn bush giving the strength of the thorn to the calf.[167]

Shaggy Head with Horns Complete: The Ooser

Just across the border, in neighbouring Dorset, an entity with cattle-like features known as the Ooser ('oose' or 'wu'se')[168] was part of country ritual and superstition. Depicted with a terrifying

---

163 The New Forest, Its Traditions, Inhabitants and Customs: De Crespigney & H Hutchinson
164 Changeling Cattle & Magical Cows: Patricia Monaghan
165 The Pattern Under the Plough: GE Evans
166 Marie Duignan, Coolronan School: National Folklore Collection
167 The Pattern Under the Plough: GE Evans
168 Glossary of Dorset: Rev. W Barnes

mask including bullock horns, cow skin and hair, and an actively snapping jaw, the Ooser scolded or made a mockery of villagers for immoral acts in a parade known as *skimmity riding*. The mask was probably mounted on a pole for the parade, as it had no eye holes to be worn as a disguise.[169] It is possible that the Ooser finds his roots in pre-Christian Britain, in the anthropomorphic old gods and winter spirits who would later come to be identified with the devil[170] (who was also depicted with bull-like features). The Ooser would become the *Christmas Bull* or the *Wooser*, a creature that was part of a similar tradition where a man masked in a hollow bull head would parade around the village and demand food and drink at Christmas, a custom that continued right up to the end of the 19th century.[171] The Ooser takes his place amongst the other somewhat macabre winter customs and superstitions of the past, when Christmas was not only a time of joy but also of retribution, trickery and death.

> *'The bull, shaggy head with horns complete, shaggy coat and eyes of glass, was wont to arrive, uninvited, at any Christmas festivity. None knew when he might or might not appear. He was given the freedom of every house, and allowed to penetrate into any room ... the whole company would flee before his formidable horns."*[172]

Today the cattle and ponies roam the Forest all year round, but this wasn't always the case. Before the Deer Removal Act of 1851 cattle and ponies stood secondary to the deer, the breeding of which remained the primary purpose for the existence of the Forest as a Royal Hunting Ground. As such, there stood a regulation in general Forest Law which stated stock should be removed from a Forest during *Fence Month* (a fortnight before and after Midsummers Day, 20th June – 20th July, when deer were fawning, *'defence'*) and *Winter Heyning* (22nd November – 4th May, when there was less forage for the deer).[173] Kenchington[174] points

---

169 'The Ooser' Somerset & Dorset Notes & Queries 1891: Charles Herbert Mayo
170 Dorset Up-Along and Down-Along: Marianna Dacombe
171 The Meaning of Witchcraft: Gerald Gardner
172 Dorset Up-Along and Down-Along: Marianna Dacombe
173 The New Forest: Horace Hutchinson
174 The Commoners New Forest: FE Kenchington

out that this regulation was not generally put into practice here, however it was introduced for a time after the deer were removed; not for the sake of the deer of course but as the primary Crown interest in the Forest had then become timber, presumably to protect young saplings. At any rate, by 1877 restrictions were removed and stock could again roam all year.

SHEEP ON THE NEW FOREST

Unlike the nearby counties of Dorset and Wiltshire, sheep are a rare sight in the New Forest. This is because in general, sheep are not commonable animals and ancient rights are held by very few. Grazing rights for sheep were only granted in special circumstances and only to favoured landowners.[175] One of these was Beaulieu Abbey, which was granted rights to properties under its control[176] and extended to the commoners who held tenancy there. These properties were not just in the area of Beaulieu village but also in Brockenhurst and Boldre villages, plus other places[177] where wool was produced and traded. Wool was an important commodity, although much like the changeling fairy-cattle whose flesh should never be eaten, many who worked with sheep considered it taboo to take a fleece from a sheep which had unexpectedly and suddenly died.[178]

In ancient times the enemy of the shepherd was of course the wolf, which in old Forest Law was sometimes counted as one of the ancient *Beasts of Venery*; an animal that could be hunted in the Forest along with others such as deer, wild boar, marten and hare. Once prolific in Britain, they were hunted largely for the purpose of elimination to prevent the loss of livestock. Magic was also used to protect livestock from harm, both here and elsewhere in Europe. A 15th century German manuscript gives a herdsman's charm appealing to the Saints to protect their sheep and cattle from wolves and foxes,

---

175 The Commoners New Forest: FE Kenchington
176 The New Forest, Its Traditions, Inhabitants and Customs: De Crespigney & H Hutchinson
177 The Commoners New Forest: FE Kenchington
178 Changeling Cattle & Magical Cows: Patricia Monaghan

'...throat of wolf and vixen block
Blood from shedding, bone from crunching...
Keep my herd from all wood-hounds!'[179]

There is no specific sheep breed associated with the New Forest, and all sorts can be seen roaming here, generally however, hardier moorland and mountain sheep are chosen, such as the Welsh Mountain Badger-Face.

---

179 Grimm: Teutonic Mythology

HEARTH, HOME
& MAGICAL MARKS

THE ONE NIGHT HOUSE

In the very heart of the New Forest...with wood fires it is
wide old fireplaces. The wind may sigh and sough in the trees,
but it does not whistle down the chimneys, so snugly does it
nestle, and all over broods the contented spirit of home.

'Lavender Thatch', from The Enchanted Forest,
Gladys M Forbes

The New Forest belonged to the Crown, together with large
estates of land and property granted by the Crown to aristocratic
Lords who in turn rented properties and farmsteads to local
people. The private estates managed business on their own land,
whilst Officers and Keepers were appointed to manage the land
directly controlled by the Crown. With much of the soil too poor
to cultivate, many families survived or supplemented their income
by grazing animals on the moors and collecting materials through
the customary (and at that time, unwritten) Rights of Common.
Many also took the opportunity to create their own homes on the
Forest, new cottages and holdings built without any official
consent by way of a tradition known in rural lore as the 'One
Night House'.

'In one or two places, whole villages sprung up in
mushroom-like fashion.[180]

Gilpin states these projects were usually carried out on a
moonlit night[181] lending the name 'moonlight-house' to these
cottages. The One Night House was essentially a type of squatting
– something that the author H Hutchinson[182] describes as *'faits*
accomplis' that is, the use of an illegal act to acquire an apparent
legal title.

---

180 The New Forest, Its Traditions, Inhabitants and Customs: De Crespigney & H
Hutchinson
181 Remarks on Forest Scenery: William Gilpin
182 The New Forest: Horace Hutchinson

RU Sayce writes in the Folklore Journal in 1942:

> *'The intending squatter ... assembled building materials*
> *near the spot ... this was done secretly. One evening at dusk*
> *they would meet together and start building. Four simple*
> *walls did not take long. Then the roof was put on ...*
> *windows were not necessary but the entrance had to be secured*
> *by a door. Then as dawn was breaking, a fire was lit on the*
> *hearth and the smoke issuing from the chimney was evidence*
> *that the work was completed and a new house established.'*[183]

Cottages were typical to the New Forest and built for function - vernacular styles[184] which drew upon easily obtainable materials and local customs. First the foundations were laid, usually a low plinth of hearthstone or brick.[185] Protective amulets are likely to have been placed under the foundations, as protection measures but also as foundation sacrifices.[186] Then the walls would be built. Although traditional New Forest cottages are usually made of cob (*'clob'*, *'korb'* or *'clay daubins'*, a material made up of local clay mixed with turf, chopped straw and heather), building with cob is a lengthy process, so it is unlikely that cob was used for the initial construction. Instead, the cottages would probably have been constructed out of timber,[187] with the frames first lifted into position (a heavy job that often involved the help of neighbours, in an occasion sometimes referred to as house *'raising'* or *'rearing'* or the *'setting of the house upon the ground'*),[188] then built up with woven *vert* (branches, sticks and twigs), followed by wattle and daub applied to finish the outside.[189] A roof was then crudely thatched.

---

183 The One Night House & its Distribution: RU Sayce (Folklore Journal, 1942)
184 Illustrated Handbook of Vernacular Architecture: RW Brunskill
185 East Boldre, A New Forest Squatters Settlement: Jude James
186 Archaeology of Ritual & Magic (Zoom Lecture) Brian Hoggard 18.04.20
187 Vernacular Architecture in the New Forest: Jude James (Hampshire Field Club report no. 15)
188 The Pattern Under The Plough: George Ewart Evans
189 Parts of a Cottage: Sidney H Heath

Protection of Property & Traditions of Ownership

At this point, more protective amulets could be placed within the walls and main timbers of the structure. Amulets were always placed in key places (both hidden and visible) in the home that could be used as a place of entry for malignant forces, such as fireplaces and door and window frames. They also underwent a sort of 'activation' at the time they were laid such as being bent, burnt, rubbed or spat upon. There are several examples of amulets collected from the New Forest and surrounding areas that may have been laid at this stage; for instance, the dart-shaped belemnite fossil (known in folk tradition as a *thunderbolt*) used to protect the household against malevolence that was collected from a property in nearby Dorset in 1985.[190] Holed-stones (or 'hag stones') were also common, such as one collected from a rural property in nearby Cranborne Chase in 1884. This particular example was nailed to the door frame and reported by the occupant to protect against Pixies.[191] In the north of the New Forest, these stones were nailed onto cottage walls and animal sheds to give protection in particular against fire, lightening, famine, plague and other evil occurrences. For the same reason, New Forest children would thread them onto a cord and wear them as necklaces or bracelets[192], and in the New Forest villages of Abbots Well and Frogham, several cottages had hag stones fixed to their walls as late as the 1960's.[193] The stones were also considered to have healing properties and when left in the moonlight for three nights could endow the wearer with improved health.[194] It seems crops were also protected by the stones and (again in Frogham) a giant necklace of stones threaded onto a piece of wire was hung between two ancient apple trees,[195] presumably to protect the garden produce.

---

190 Collected in Dorset, 1985 - now in the Pitt Rivers Museum, Oxford (1985.51.837)
191 Collected at Cranborne Chase, 1884 - now in the Pitt Rivers Museum, Oxford (1884.56.3)
192 The Folklore of Hampshire & the Isle of Wight: Wendy Boase
193 Wanderers in the New Forest, Juliette de Bairacli Levy
194 The Folklore of Hampshire & the Isle of Wight: Wendy Boase
195 Wanderers in the New Forest, Juliette de Bairacli Levy

Man-made amulets were also used in the area, such as dolls and figures made in wax, possibly either to represent the occupants themselves or lost relatives. These sorts of figures might also have been used in a warding sense; depicting a person who the occupant either wanted to control or repel from the property. Another interesting object was found in Christchurch; a small coffin made out of a heavy metal and inscribed with a name.[196] It is also possible that the folk-custom of burying horse skulls was carried out in Hampshire, a common practice elsewhere in the UK. Although at the time of writing I could find no examples of horse skull burials in the New Forest, its more than possible this practice may have been alive here, where the horse was such a big part of daily life and superstition. Skulls were believed to repel malign forces and vermin from the property and to offer protection from malign spirits such as the *mare*, a horse spirit that brought bad luck and nightmares. In other cases, the skulls of particularly good horses were buried within the house in order to retain their good nature.[197] Horse skulls for these protective purposes have been found both under the foundations of properties and also under the flagstones in front of the fire[198] and hung in rafters or above entrances.[199] In other parts of the British Isles, they were also buried under floors to enhance the sounds of music.[200]

Once the fire was lit in the hearth, the work was done. Often, the build was a communal venture for a family or newly-weds and once the work was completed everyone involved would *hansel* the cottage by dancing on the wet clay floor.[201] The cottage would eventually be discovered by the Keepers but when they were, a most unusual thing happened - they were often allowed to stay. The tenants found themselves charged a fine but were otherwise allowed to remain in exchange for a rent under a rather cryptic

---

196 Collected in Christchurch, 1998 - now in the Pitt Rivers Museum, Oxford (1998.42.1)
197 The Pattern Under The Plough: George Ewart Evans
198 Archaeology of Ritual & Magic (Zoom Lecture) Brian Hoggard 18.04.20
199 Traditional Witchcraft, A Cornish Book of Ways: Gemma Gary
200 The Pattern Under The Plough: George Ewart Evans
201 'House in Time' ABE Project 1997 – Project outline

tenancy known as *Keyhold Tenure*. Later on (once residency was assured) the wooden walls would be reworked or extended with cob, creating the typical New Forest cob cottage, which from personal experience I can say is surprisingly warm in the winter and cool in the summer.

TYPICAL NEW FOREST COB COTTAGE, FROGHAM (CIRCA 300 YEARS OLD) HOME TO AUTHOR JULIETTE DE BAIRACLI LEVY ('WANDERERS OF THE NEW FOREST') AND LATER OWNED BY AUTHOR IRENE SOPER ('NEW FOREST COOKERY')

There were several requirements laid out in New Forest folk-tradition to assure residency in a newly built One-Night-House under Keyhold Tenure. One was that it was important to have a door in place[202] to mark the threshold of the cottage and its ownership, and we see evidence of brandings on cottage and stable doors as dwellers marked the property as their own. But arguably the most important by custom was that the hearthstone must be laid, the chimney built and the fire burning in the hearth by dawn, with smoke seen visibly coming out of the chimney.[203] Not only was the hearth a source of warmth that also enabled families to cook, but it was also the heart of the home. The hearth was seen as sacred, a symbol of home and community - a place of worship where apotropaic marks could be carved and amulets could be hidden, tying protective spirits to the house. This was also the case in a Christian context, with fireplaces and hearth

202 The One Night House & its Distribution: RU Sayce (Folklore Journal, 1942)
203 The History of England VI: Peter Ackroyd

lintels in Hampshire etched with Christian house blessings in Latin.[204]

RW Brunskill writes:

> *'It is impossible to exaggerate the significance of the hearth in the design of vernacular houses ... it has been suggested that the house began as a shelter for fire and that it was fire that made the house sacred.'*[205]

Despite not being legally binding, its customary authority is clear; fire has historically been used as a mark of ownership if only in folk-custom and common lore. Grimm tells us that across Europe, *'the kindling and maintaining of the fire upon real estate was proof of its lawful occupation and possession.'*[206]

Signs remain of the fascinating history of these cob cottages and their hearths, such as the aforementioned brandings and evil-averting cut-marks on the lintels above the fireplaces, which offered both a source of heat and a method of cooking, often with ancient worn hearthstones, in-built baking ovens and areas to hang meats. In other rural parts of Britain there is a firm belief in protective chimney spirits, such as *Old Clim* of East Anglia[207] and it's very possible that a similar belief was held by people of the New Forest. Given the New Forest's intimate relationship with horses, Clim's connections to the blacksmith trade make this particularly feasible and the spirit of Clim could be tied to the property with brand marks made by the occupier. Brian Hoggard writes[208] that not only was the hearth seen as a sacred place but also a point of vulnerability (as were other points of entry, such as windows and doors). As such, the hearth needed to be protected from volatile spirits that might be drawn down the chimney, especially if elder was being burnt – elder being believed in Hampshire to attract devilish spirits to your hearth. As James I writes in his 1597 *Daemonologie,*

---

204 Hampshire Houses 1250-1700: Edward Roberts (contribution by Linda Hall)
205 Traditional Buildings of Britain: RW Brunskill
206 Journal of the Derbyshire Archaeological & History Society, 1907
207 Secrets of East Anglian Magic: Nigel Pennick
208 Magical House Protection, The Archaeology of Counter-Witchcraft: Brian Hoggard

'...being transformed in the likeness of a little beast or
fowl, they will come and pierce through whatever house or
church, though all ordinary passages may be closed, by
whatever open(ing) air might enter at.'

Cut, burn and brand marks not only marked ownership of a property but also offered protection and longevity, with symbols often progressively added over time by generations of the family, reinforcing their meaning. Some of these old cob buildings even come with their own *fire churms* which should not be removed from the house - such as commoner branding irons, or bends of leather branded with the symbols of the family who inhabited the cottage. In the Green Dragon pub in Brook, there still remains such bends of leather. Incidentally the Green Dragon also still holds another old tradition, the right to the ancient measure of two *'cords'* of Forest wood per year (1 'cord' is equal to 4ft x 4ft x 8ft).

Due to the hearth being the customary factor indicating occupancy, the commoning rights of *Turbary* and *Estovers* - to take peat and timber from the Forest for fuel were originally attached to the chimney and hearth of a cottage rather than a person or entire property. They are now obsolete, but Sumner writes[209] that should a house be pulled down or altered in any way, the chimney must be left standing otherwise the property would lose its rights. De Crespigney & Hutchinson tell us,

'it is for this reason we sometimes see in the Forest a
fireplace curiously situated in a cabbage bed or an orchard,
with no apparent function or reason for its existence. It stands
there in witness of its right for fuel.'[210]

In the Fleur De Leys, a thatched pub in Lymington dating back to at least the 1400's (but likely much older), the original fireplace opening can still be seen in the stone-flagged entrance passage.[211] One of my many questionable pastimes when out riding is to spot these fireplaces at the bottom of gardens.

209 Cuckoo Hill, The Book of Gorley: Heywood Sumner
210 The New Forest, Its Traditions, Inhabitants and Customs: De Crespigney & H Hutchinson
211 Geoff Boel: Picturesque Pubs of the New Forest

Sometimes I see iron woodburners, surrounded with the remains of brickwork, forlorn and rusty, covered with creeping thorns and ivy. I'm not sure if these are related but they are certainly interesting curiosities. Other interesting features of New Forest supersition can be found in cottage gardens. For instance, bay and rowan were often planted by the garden gate as they were believed to ward evil, and elder was known to be lucky when planted near the house, although unlucky elsewhere (and sometimes considered to cause delirium).[212] We also often see very old hawthorn bushes left to grow around properties, possibly due to the belief that fairies lived within them. This was especially the case for lone hawthorns, standing in the middle of moorland:

> '...a solitary thorn tree ... these are considered to be bewitched. They should be carefully avoided at night, as a fiery wheel will come forth and if a person does not make a hasty retreat, he will be destroyed.[213]

The tradition of the One-Night-House was such an ancient folk practice that despite not being supported legally, it was generally believed to be common law; as Sayce writes, 'with no other sanction than the common feeling that it was just 'right'.[214] Beyond the folk-tradition that reinforced it, the reality was that it was a lengthy process to evict a person inhabiting a house. It was more cost-effective for the authorities to start charging rent or grant a leasehold instead. The exact conditions for the 'tenancies' were sketchy. For instance in Hampshire, it was understood that the occupiers had no right to sell these homes (or to will them away) but instead, it was believed that on the tenant dying the first person to cross the threshold took their place as the rightful tenant.[215] Rightful by custom perhaps, but legally, just another squatter. Author and archaeologist Heywood Sumner writing in the 1900's (after the Act of 1800 had been passed) tells us that 'the usual custom was to grant such squatters a lease of his holding for three lives

---

212 The Forest in Folklore & Mythology: Alexander Porteous
213 Northern Mythology: Thorpe
214 The One Night House & its Distribution: RU Sayce (Folklore Journal, 1942)
215 The London Globe 1907

at a nominal rental.[216] An *Erection of Cottages Act* was issued in 1588 which attempted to eradicate Keyhold Tenure – however, it endured. And in 1698, the status of all existing properties within the New Forest and their associated rights became officially recorded in the *Atlas of Rights* - but still, it appears the custom continued. Then in the early 1800's the New Forest Commission was appointed to look into encroachments on the Forest by an Act of Parliament *(Act for the Better Preservation of Timber in the New Forest)* and all Forest land was surveyed and encroachments marked. Any 'rogue' buildings and small pieces of enclosed land that remained in-situ for 15 years or more were granted either a leasehold or a freehold, or otherwise reclaimed as Forest land, and in 1854 the commoning rights held by any property (which were previously customary rights, and not written down) were recorded and listed in the *'Register of Claims to Rights over the Forest'*.[217] Following this, all new encroachments were considered illegal and liable for prosecution.[218] Despite this, despite a detailed record existing of what had been built and what land enclosed, it wasn't uncommon for the tenant to gradually extend their home and land, little by little. It was an offence known in the Forest as *purpresture* or *assart* (depending on the circumstances) but usually so imperceptible that it was rare to be caught out. A common way to surreptitiously extend a property in the New Forest was to move your fence a few foot by night and immediately release pigs onto the new section to root up the soil, making a mess of the ground and thereby covering up the evidence. Even today, the ancient Court of Verderers still work towards challenging new encroachments thus preserving the traditions and delicate ecosystems that the New Forest supports.

---

216 Cuckoo Hill, The Book of Gorley: Heywood Sumner
217 With thanks to Sylvia Crocker: Netley Marsh History Group
218 With thanks to Sylvia Crocker: Netley Marsh History Group

MAGICAL MARKS IN THE NEW FOREST

Protection & Empowerment: Public Spaces & the Home

Although buildings in the New Forest were essentially designed with practicality in mind, there are a number of interesting features which also hint at protective and evil-averting functions. One of these are *apotropaic* symbols; charms carved into buildings during their construction or at various times during the habitation of the building, often over a period of several hundred years. The charms can be found on fireplace mantels, ceiling beams, door and window frames, and other focal points inside the property. At Waterditch Cottage in Poulner, Ringwood (dating to 1685) horizontal 'cat-scratch' apotropaic 'mesh marks' can be found on the window mullions.[219] Here, the purpose of the charm was to confuse malign spirits who, it was believed, would follow and become confused by continuous or repetitive lines. Just outside the New Forest at Grove Place in Nursling, we find a similar charm made up of a number of intersecting and parallel lines; again, acting as a spirit trap and repeller.

The purpose of the apotropaic mark varied depending on the symbol used and where it was positioned, but in general it acted to disperse malign influences; they were evil-averting symbols believed to repel and ward off evil spirits. Some etchings, such as ladder and mesh patterns (## i.e. crossed/intersecting lines) were intended to confuse and in some cases even capture evil spirits and considered the 'classic' witch mark.[220] However we also find a number of quite beautiful patterns, which besides a decorative function also had a magical objective, distracting spirits from their mischievous purposes.[221] Although perhaps rarer in the New Forest than some other areas of the country, the New Forest still has its fair share of these symbols in private homes and public spaces. Whilst we have to bear in mind that not all of these are apotropaic (some may be coincidental, created for practical use or simply graffiti) I can't describe how exciting it was to visit some

---

219 Hampshire Houses 1250-1700: Edward Roberts (contribution by Linda Hall)
220 Hampshire Houses 1250-1700: Edward Roberts (contribution by Linda Hall)
221 Averting Demons: Ruth Mellinkoff

of these places and discover these marks hidden in plain view. I also feel very lucky I decided to carry out this part of my research when I did (before the pandemic), as much of it would have been impossible during 2020/early 2021. I was also lucky to have my son with me, only three years old at the time, alerting me to shapes which at first I did not see!

INGLENOOK FIREPLACE AT THE ROYAL OAK, FRITHAM

Old pubs are a natural place to find apotropaic marks, in many ways being an extension of the home and as such needing similar spiritual protection. In The Royal Oak in Fritham, which dates to the 15th century, there are a multitude of marks on the fireplace and also on the ceiling beams. There are parallel 'cat-scratch' marks here similar to those found in Poulner. Other marks include several of the so-called 'Marion' marks - 'VV' or 'MM' etchings, known as the Virgin Mary charm and in folk-belief representing life, death and fertility. Integrated with one of these Marion charms there are is also another combination of symbols which could be interpreted as four small pony hoofprints. Given the setting, the strangely formed Marion mark itself that encloses them could be a deer hoof print instead; or perhaps a Kings Mark – either way, all significant links to commoning and Forest life. A similar one can be seen at the Verderers Court in Lyndhurst, and in The Swan Inn just outside Lyndhurst we find more Marion charms and parallel 'cat-scratches', or 'mesh marks', in an old beam above the fireplace, dating as early as the 1700's. Care should be taken to consider however, that some haphazard cuts like these on lintels could be 'face marks' which were the result of preparing wood for plaster). One of the most intriguing finds so far in the New Forest may be at Queens House in Lyndhurst, which adjoins the Verderers Court.[222] Here we find a half-finished hexafoil (otherwise known as the *Daisy Wheel*) in the oak mantel of the library room fireplace. Some lovely examples can also be found at St Mary's Church in Fordingbridge, where a large unfinished hexafoil is etched into the main porch, whilst inside, four beautiful interlocking hexafoils are etched into an internal door surround. This example also has a pentagram carved into the opposite wall; pentagrams are often found in churches by doorways, possibly to protect from intrusion by malignant entities.[223]

Hexafoils in the New Forest

The hexafoil was used for distracting and possibly containing spirits; it was also considered a magical amulet, having six arms symbolic of totality and the 'centre' of all things. Its origins can be found in pre-history, where it was originally a solar symbol and believed to illuminate dark places on the ethereal plane[224]. It would later be used as a symbol of devotion as a Christogram. As researcher Richard Kemp explains,[225] the Medieval mind imagined the universe as a fixed circle of stars which contained the sun, the moon and the planets. Mary was invoked as 'Queen of Heaven', so not only does the circular pattern represent the

---

222 With thanks to Andrew Norris at team of Planning & Heritage, Forestry England
223 Some Apotropaic Marks in the church of St Mary the Virgin, Fordingbridge: Richard Kemp, 2017
224 Brian Hoggard, private correspondence
225 Some Apotropaic Marks in the church of St Mary the Virgin, Fordingbridge: Richard Kemp, 2017

universe but also the female divinity herself as *Auspice Maria*, 'Protector'. Of course the hexafoil was older than its Christian origins and together with its predecessors, was already well established as a symbol to conjure the protection of both the sun and a feminine higher power. As such, the hexafoil was often used in conjunction with Marion-marks.[226]

But if this symbol evoked the protection of a feminine higher power, then who was etching it into the walls of churches and wooden fireplaces? Until recently, scholars assumed hexafoil patterns had been created by (male) stone mason students, who were practising with their compass. However, this theory has now largely been discounted. Firstly, there can have been no benefit for an intelligent student of architecture to repeat this pattern (and only this pattern!) over and over again. Secondly, the sizes of the hexafoils raise a question; as many are much larger than the capacity of a compass. Thirdly, the symbol is often found in domestic settings etched into wood - outside of the stone mason's territory. Researchers are now convinced that these patterns were in fact made by another tool – women's fabric shears. Fabric and wool shears were a common tool of women, both in and prior to the medieval period and depicted hanging from women's belts in medieval paintings and tapestries.[227] The connections between the hexafoil and womankind, both as 'Mary the Protector', her guises in older pre-Christian female spirits, and the symbols' purpose as a 'light-bringer', make this theory very convincing. Large numbers of this symbol are found etched on and around baptism fonts, suggesting the symbol was used in the protection of infants and their mothers. It was also used as a decoration on domestic furniture such as wooden blanket boxes, where it was believed to offer protection against theft. The hexafoils we find in churches and private homes alike signify the blending of old and new spiritualities - folk-beliefs and practices adapting to the state religion and common themes enduring. A divinity honoured differently - but consistently - by common folk. The symbol

---

226 Archaeology of Ritual & Magic (Zoom Lecture) Brian Hoggard 18.04.20
227 Medieval Graffiti: Matthew Champion

offered the protection of the sun and solar powers, of a female divinity and was the women's opportunity to create a lasting presence in their homes and churches.

More examples of hexafoils in the New Forest area can be seen at Christchurch Priory including four consecutive daisy wheels - again, with an accompanying pentagram. Just outside of the New Forest boundaries, at King John's House in Romsey, we find a beautifully intricate hexafoil with four interlocking daisy wheels and an even more elaborate symbol in a flower representation of the sun, which has 12 petals and can be found on the north wall. The hexafoil was known to bring solar protective qualities in the form of the sunburst. Several variations of hexafoils appear to act as sun charms, some with eight spokes and possibly also symbolising the agricultural year such as the one at St Mary's Church at Carisbrooke on the nearby Isle of Wight. They were also used as directional compass points, with hexafoils being positioned within buildings at north, south, east and west - perhaps to consecrate and protect the area within their boundaries, such as the examples at St Cross Hospital in nearby Winchester.[228]

Hexafoils have also been found carved into trees in the New Forest, together with a range of other tree-carved symbols (known as *arbor glyphs*) and although these are harder to date, the examples found so far in the New Forest are likely to be at least 100 years old. The New Forest has the largest number of ancient trees in south western Europe[229] and new glyphs are being found all the time. The New Forest National Park Authority are currently running a public-led survey of ancient tree graffiti which you can view at www.newforestnpa.gov.uk/tree-graffiti/

228 Hampshire Houses 1250-1700, Edward Roberts (contribution by Linda Hall)
229 Lawrence Shaw, Archaeological Officer New Forest National Park Authority

RITUALISTIC BURN MARKS AT QUEENS HOUSE, LYNDHURST

Back at Queens House in Lyndhurst, etchings include a possible stirrup iron and eyelet/hook impression marks, ladder/fencing etchings and also ritualistic burn marks which are believed to have been used in the protection of buildings from fire, amongst other uses (such as the 'ghost candle', shining light on the ethereal plane so darkness cannot gather in that spot, similar to the function of the daisy wheel[230]). There is also an **XX** symbol which may of course have been intended as a Roman numeral but which again, as a symbol, had older folk meanings.[231] In the adjoining Verderers Court we also find a wooden witness box/dock which is carved with countless initials and symbols; no doubt some apotropaic and others signifying the initials of those making court appearances. We also find chevron-etchings and wheel-marks ⊕ known as the 'suncross', an ancient sun symbol later used as a consecration mark in churches. This symbol could also be interpreted as a hunting 'target' glyph, given the setting. There are also a number of so-called Marion marks, some of which could possibly, given their shape, be interpreted as deer or cattle hoof prints. A similar one can be seen at The Royal Oak pub in Fritham, which was also closely linked to commoning and hunting.

Old buildings in the New Forest have revealed other interesting markings such as carpenter marks or shipping marks,

---

230 Brian Hoggard, personal correspondence
231 Thanks to Andrew Norris of Forestry England for taking photos of these when my visit had to be cancelled at the start of the pandemic.

made with an implement known as a 'timber scribe' which identified timbers and indicated construction details when the wood was cut at the yard. Some are crude and others detailed, but they are almost always found at the joints/ends of beams and accompanied with Roman numerals.[232] Although we might initially be disappointed that these symbols are not apotropaic, they are really interesting in their own right as each mark was unique to the trader and was often used as a means of personal identification, being engraved on rings and used for witnessing documents.[233] They also resemble mason marks: precisely carved symbols which identified the master builder behind the design and construction of a property. As such, they may have had some ceremonial significance surrounding the construction of the building. Although they cannot be classed as true 'witch-marks', George Ewart Evans writes that early masons undoubtedly adapted apotropaic and pagan markings with ritual and magical significance.[234]

Witch Marks

The term 'witch-mark' can be misleading as it suggests the marks were created *by* or *against* witches - but in fact it refers to the belief that the marks repelled malign forces and bad luck of all sorts, and not solely conceived to ward off just witchcraft[235]. By comparison, witch bottles, created in the mid-third quarter of the seventeenth century, specifically aimed to control negative forces *assumed* as spirit 'witches' - often made using Bartmann or 'Bellarmine' jugs (ceramic jars with a bearded face on the side, some of which have been found in fragments on private land in and around the New Forest). As Professor Ronald Hutton discusses in both his books *The Triumph of the Moon* and *The Witch*, during the medieval period the concept of the witch was very much imagined as a malign supernatural spirit - quite separate from the cunning man or woman who worked with magic *against*

232 Hampshire Houses 1250-1700: Edward Roberts (contribution by Linda Hall)
233 The Pattern Under The Plough: George Ewart Evans
234 The Pattern Under The Plough: George Ewart Evans
235 Brian Hoggard, personal correspondence

the very spirits considered as 'witches'. These individuals were more often than not embraced by the community and in many cases even identified as Christians themselves. Religion and magic were not so clearly distinguished as they are today, and protection marks were made by both cunning magic-workers and the lay person with knowledge of local folk-superstition, in a spiritual battleground of 'magic versus magic'.

Magical Warfare in New Forest Churches

The power of apotropaic marks and magical symbols was timeless and hard to resist; as such they also played a part in deflecting evil spirits out of churches. Many of the marks found in old churches are on the southern-side of inner walls and pillars facing towards the north - a place associated with the devil (or perhaps more accurately, the land spirits and ancient gods that came to be considered as or conflated with malign spirits and daemons). The northern side of a churchyard, for instance, became an undesirable place to be buried and Lady Chapels and altars to female Saints were usually situated in the north of the church because women were generally held in some suspicion. An example of this northerly deflection can be found in the St Mary's Church in Fordingbridge which dates from the 12th century, where a plethora of symbols include daisy wheels, a pentagram and an eight-spoked star, symbolising balance and the compass points of the spirit world (north, south, east, west and above and below).[236] We also find demon-like characters carved into the walls of St Mary's, reminiscent of the daemons depicted in the PGM (Greek Magical Papyri) who face towards the north.[237]

In all forms of 'sympathetic' magic, images are created of the person, animal or being that the magic-worker aims to control. The same applied in medieval folk-magic, with the intent to control demons and malign spirits within churches. Whilst it may seem counter-intuitive to etch images of demonic spirits onto the

---

236 Caution should be taken interpreting this symbol as it can also be a carpenters' mark indicating a centre point.
237 With thanks to researchers Richard Kemp & Aldous Rees, Hampshire Medieval Graffiti Survey

walls of a church, the purpose was to depict what they feared in an attempt to control its existence. In the case of St Mary's, the demon-like beings face the north, where they stand for and represent the malign spirits who will be deflected out of the church (or denied entry). According to the author Matthew Champion[238] the significance of demons might also be representing the 'consequence of sin'. The etching of the demons on the wall could be a reminder of what awaits those who have committed sin, or, equally, an attempt to appease the demons who the unfortunate person believes they have conjured by their sinful actions. Daemon-like characters have also been found carved onto trees in the New Forest, such as the below found near Burley; image with thanks to The New Forest National Park Authority's Tree Graffiti Survey.

DAEMON-LIKE FIGURE CARVED INTO A TREE NEAR BURLEY

238 Medieval Graffiti: Matthew Champion

In St Mary's we also find the lightning strike, found here and elsewhere in the New Forest, which was thought to protect from lightning and ward off storms. According to folklore, lightning never strikes twice; therefore, in a similar way to warding off demons by drawing them, etching a lightning strike onto a building means that the property was considered already 'struck' and therefore protected.[239] St Mary's also has carvings of boats and fish and hash # and ladder etchings (spirit traps), amongst other magical markings. Another interesting feature at Fordingbridge Church is the so-called Knights Templar Anointing Stone; a large piece of stone (probably ironstone) set into the outer southern wall and deeply incised with blade marks. It is also known locally as the 'miracle stone' and continued to be cut by local people beyond the Templar period for healing purposes. There are also a number of apotropaic marks that can be found around the stone, perhaps made in an exchange for using the site or to 'set in stone' the intent to heal the sick person - a 'prayer made solid'. Inside the church etchings of crossed swords and shield shapes can also be seen: heraldic inscriptions or perhaps linked to the Templar history.

'FAIRY DOOR' AT ST MICHAEL'S CHURCH, SOPLEY

---

239 Medieval Graffiti: Matthew Champion

It is possible that the apotropaic marks found in churches worked hand in hand with so-called 'devil doors' (unusually small or bricked-up church doors). It was generally understood that these doors were found on the northern wall and accounts exist of these doors being opened during ceremonies such as baptisms to ensure malign spirits had a clear exit, to 'flee' towards the 'pagan' direction of north. If this is the case, apotropaic marks made facing the north would have acted as a catalyst for this, much like marks found on windowframes and fireplaces in domestic settings would have repelled spirits out of the home as well as blocking them from coming in. It is also reported that when the churches were first built on pagan ground, the north door acted as an entrance both for those newly converting to Christianity, being people who would have been familiar with entering sacred spaces by the north, and others known as 'leper squints', those who were contagiously sick and perhaps seen as ungodly. As folk-history would have it, post-Reformation the larger doors were bricked-up to *'prevent the superstition lingering'*.[240] The theory of the devil door is now generally discounted, in many cases due to church orientations and other practical considerations but largely just because the accounts are not sourced. It is an interesting possibility though; because as the marks suggest, just because something isn't officially documented doesn't mean it didn't exist in the lives of the ordinary lay-person. Symbols and customs used by the common person just don't appear within mainstream records. Nicholas Groves writes in his paper *Devil's Doors Revisited* [241] (which I should mention, largely aims to discount the devil-door theory): *'This is not to say that north doors were not left open at baptisms - but that if they were, it was a piece of folk-religion, and definitely not part of the official liturgy.'*

These features are also known as 'fairy doors' in the New Forest. The word fairy refers to the trickster spirits so important in local New Forest superstition and conflated with the 'devil' via

---

240 Devil's Doors Revisited: Nicholas Groves, 2015
241 Devil's Doors Revisited: Nicholas Groves, 2015

the Old English *deofol*: 'a false god or subordinate spirit.'[242] A notable northerly-sealed door in the New Forest can be found at the 13th century St Mary's Church in Ellingham. It also has a stunning blue and gilt sundial over the southerly entrance, and also boasts a sunburst apotropaic symbol on the south wall similar to one found in St Mary's Church in Carisbrooke (Isle of Wight). Ellingham Church also has a mason mark symbol (known as benchmark) on the eastern wall. Another New Forest church with a northerly-sealed door is the incredibly old St Mary's Breamore Church which dates back to the Saxon times, around 1000AD, which is also known for its Anglo-Saxon inscriptions and wall paintings. There are in fact two doors – a blocked 19th century door and an older porch and doorway dating to at least the 15th century, both in the north. Unfortunately, the church needed major indoor restoration and the modern plastering has almost certainly covered up apotropaic marks that may have existed inside. However there are some mason marks on the outside southerly wall and some folk-marks on the porch walls and medieval font. It has a noticeable '**x**' on the internal door latch, a folk symbol meaning 'legacy' and often found on latches with the possible intention of averting malevolence entering. This can also be seen above doors and on lintels, as well as etched directly onto the wall, such as at Minstead Church. Outside, there is an ancient yew tree in the churchyard which thrives despite its hollow trunk. Although its exact age is unknown, it was almost certainly already a mature tree when the church was first built over a thousand years ago.[243] The planting of yew was customary in churchyards across the British Isles and in the New Forest they were also planted at garden gates together with holly and believed to offer protection. Bay and elder were also believed to repel evil when planted near the house, although elder was otherwise generally considered unlucky.[244] Protective qualities were also believed of rowan. It was considered almost as potent for warding evil as

---

242 Online Etymology Dictionary
243 The Saxon Church of Breamore: Anthony Light & Gerald Ponting
244 The Folklore of Hampshire & the Isle of Wight: Wendy Boase

iron,[245] with a particular ability to neutralise the power of a witch (or otherwise causing them to be carried off by the devil).[246] An ancient Northumbrian verse from the 1200's describes the neutralising effect of rowan on witches:

> *Their spells were in vain, the boys returned,*
> *To the Queen in a sorrowful mood.*
> *Crying that "witches have no power*
> *Where there is rowan-tree wood!"*[247]

A sealed door can also be found at St Mary's Church in Hale. This church is relatively new, only built in the 1700's, but a church has stood on the site since at least the 14th century. It is built on what could easily be described as a tor, a blustery high point above the River Avon which is accessed by a twisting, steep country road and then by foot, up a very steep footpath. The sealed door here is in the south. The whole area seems to be rather special, and whilst this is conjecture, it was perhaps a sacred spot for our ancestors. A short way back down the hill is a strange conical brick structure which covers Picket Well, which is fed by underground streams from the Forest. There is also a circular mound called Windmill Ball, a Bronze Age barrow,[248] and a substantial oak tree by the roadside at Fish Ponds Bottom called the *Gally Hunter*. The origin of the name is uncertain, but the author and local historian Gerald Goff recorded that *Galli-Bagger* was a local New Forest term for 'scarecrow'.[249]

Another New Forest church probably built on a sacred site is the 13th century Church of St Michael in Sopley. This church is another reminder of our ancient pagan past and, like Hale, is built right next to the River Avon on a tor-like mound, which according to Heywood Sumner was *'sacred to the Celts'*.[250] Again, there is evidence inside St Michael's of both apotropaic marks and mason marks, but the church has undergone much restoration

---

245 The Pattern Under the Plough: George Ewart Evans
246 The Forest in Folklore & Mythology: Alexander Porteous
247 The Laidly Worm of Spindleston Heugh
248 Churches of the New Forest: B&G Peckham
249 History of Hale: Gerald Goff
250 The Book of Gorley: Heywood Sumner

and the internal walls have been plastered over, covering up other apotropaic marks that almost certainly existed there. Generally, this church and its grounds are positively weird - from the moment we arrived my compass was confused and I found myself walking round and round the church not quite sure which angle I was looking at. There are also some interesting marks at the nearby 17th-century building in Sopley, now the Woolpack Inn but originally a private domestic house. Here we can find two large ceiling beams, both showing parallel and intersecting lines. The meaning behind these has been debated - some believe they are carpenter marks but, from my perspective, the marks seem too large to be a carpenters' marks, and too impulsively created – they seem almost creatively 'slashed' into the wood. Their position on the beam is also central, which does not fit the usual carpenters' mark.

Minstead Church is also worth a visit, with beautiful old yew trees and a *clootie-tree*. Here, we find a Marion-mark VV on the pew, a mark created out of tiny consecutive circles (possibly pin marks) and a 'mesh' spirit trap etching on the outer wall. There are also **xx** etchings, a glyph that anciently symbolised 'legacy'. The **xx** glyph is relatively common in graffiti surveys and the New Forest is no exception. **X** as a magical or spiritual glyph can also be seen at Poulner Farmhouse in Butlers Lane. And in St Mary's Church in Eling, on the eastern boundaries of the Forest, it is accompanied by a pentagram. Minstead Church is also set upon a tor-like mound - as Heywood Sumner writes, *'like all the churches in the Forest, except Beaulieu.'*

The use of folk magic hand-in-hand with religion is not unusual, indeed one of the most widely recorded places to view apotropaic marks is in old churches. But why would magical symbols be found in a church? To understand, we need to explore some of the history behind these folk customs. The medieval state religion of Catholicism had in many ways been similar to some of the most successful ancient religions of the world in terms of both expression and celebration. Indeed, many folk customs and rituals made their way into the underlying feel of the Catholic church, including a touch of superstition, and it too embraced a degree of earthly pleasures to enhance the religious experience - such as grand festivals, scents, colour, art, and ornamentation. Today it can be difficult for us to spot historical graffiti on plain church walls, but in the Medieval period they were far from being hidden, being etched into brightly coloured walls, revealing the pale stone beneath and bursting with colour for all to see. Although this folk custom was never part of mainstream church practice, it was seen as perfectly acceptable by the church, who both advocated and made use of them. One example is the number of daisy wheels which can be found etched on and around church fonts, even appearing in the design of the fonts themselves, placed there to protect and bless children who were being baptized in them.

But in the 16th century came the Reformation, which marked the early beginnings of the Protestant church. The Protestants aimed to reinterpret the teachings of the Bible, make religion more accessible to the masses, and bring an end to the practice of indulgence - in this context, a corruption that had developed whereby someone could 'buy' forgiveness for sins, in exchange for money. The Protestants also translated the Bible out of Latin into the common tongue, so it could be understood by everybody. The Catholic Church had become so powerful and held such a monopoly over the running of the country that it had become corrupt on many levels, and the Reformation aimed to break this hold on religious belief. They would be successful in establishing their own church, but in their zeal to overthrow corruption they also discarded a huge range of ritual paraphernalia, artwork, décor and imagery, seeing them as unnecessary cult objects and images. Unfortunately these things were not just removed but destroyed in a nazi-esque fashion; libraries were razed to the ground and churches stripped of artwork, their bright wall paintings covered over with limewash.[251]

They also aimed to cast aside superstitions such as the relics, charms and magical marks used by the community, which were all henceforth considered a form of idolatry. However, removing

---

251 Matthew Champion: Medieval Graffiti

ancient and indigenous folk-customs is not an easy task. They had existed even before the Catholic church, having simply synchronised and integrated into mainstream faith at a common level - as they always had done, reinforced by those who had an absolute and unwavering belief in their power. As Matthew Champion writes in his excellent book on the subject, *Medieval Graffiti*,

> *'Disciplines of art history and medieval manuscript tend to depict only the mainstream orthodox view of the Medieval world … the imagery found scratched into our church walls tends to be at the other end of the spectrum … steeped in folklore and superstition…*
> *Graffiti inscriptions … particularly ritual protection markings, were simply too deep-rooted in local custom and belief to be swept away.'*[252]

As ritual marks were pushed out of churches, they moved into domestic settings.[253] People took their folk-practices back into their own homes, and it is from this timeframe we see more magical marks in private residences and pubs. They were located in key places such as above the hearth and on oak timbers; the old ways of worship. Just like the more ancient symbols they were derived from, the symbols etched in churches transformed yet again, becoming embraced as lucky symbols with protective qualities - such as the 'VV' or 'MM' Marion-mark etchings, whose meaning within a church setting became blurred and returned to the realms of folk-magic and superstition.

Of course, some graffiti was probably carried out just for the fun of it - like the carvings found in Ringwood Meeting House, a Grade II* listed building built in the 1700's in Meeting House Lane. Here, a perhaps otherwise forgettable naughty schoolboy named Toby used his school-time wisely to carve his own lasting mark in history on the box pews; a legacy in the form of his handprint, his own name and a comedic big-nosed illustration of his teacher, simply named 'Sir'.

---

252 Matthew Champion: Medieval Graffiti
253 Matthew Champion: Medieval Graffiti

Other Signs & Symbols

Another example of apotropaic intention are the iron wall anchors/tie plates seen on the outside of walls and used to finish the structural ironworks. Whilst the external part of the wall anchor does play some practical purpose, the designs themselves do not always offer optimum strength, which suggests that some plate designs were chosen for the sake of tradition or superstition. Anchor plates were fired by the blacksmith, who often favoured a particular folk-mark as their traditional foundry symbol, which was usually important to the local area or the craftsman themselves. In other cases, the owner of the property would request a particular symbol for the protection or apotropaic function. Iron itself was of course considered a sacred and magical material, and the Blacksmith considered an alchemist; while shaping the metal he both identified his work as his own and bestowed longevity to the house.

These decorative ironworks were made in variations of traditional folk shapes with fitting meanings behind them. Similar symbols are etched into walls and timbers, such as **X** (a folk symbol meaning 'legacy' - today considered the equivalent of the Anglo Saxon rune *Gebo*) and **S** (a folk symbol for 'warmth and joy' - today considered the equivalent of the Anglo Saxon rune *Sigel*). **S** was also associated with the pot hake (hook) that the cooking pot would be hung on above the fireplace.[254] **S** may also be related to the rune *Eoh,* considered a guardian of flame, bringing *'joy upon an estate'.*[255] **S** was sometimes reversed, or placed on its side. **X** and **S** can also be seen carved into tombstones, such as at St Mary's Church in Eling (situated just outside the eastern edge of the New Forest) together with compass-drawn circles. The *lemniscate* (meaning 'decorated with ribbons') symbol ∞ also sometimes features, and was a symbol of longevity. It can also be considered as two sideways 'S' Sigel shapes combined, or as the 'egg-timer' shape of a sideways, enclosed **X** often seen crudely

---

254 Secrets of East Anglian Magic: Nigel Pennick
255 Anglo-Saxon Rune Poem, 8th/9th century BCE

carved into wood and stone but also decoratively crafted out of metal and described in folk-graffiti studies as the 'butterfly'. This range of symbols also often feature in the edging patterns of the thatch used to roof the cob cottages of the New Forest and in wooden wall braces, which are diagonal exposed timbers on the outside of walls.

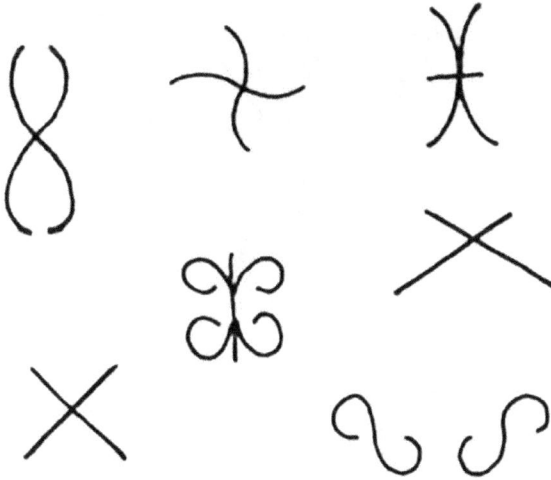

VARIOUS WALL PLATES

In later buildings we also see these symbols painted onto the brick with tar, or created by different coloured bricks used to build the design into the wall itself. Symbols were either painted onto the building when it was built or added at a later date by families wanting to add their personal 'mark' on the property. The purpose can be twofold; a decorative feature but also a symbolic folk tradition, in particular diamond shapes and ⚯ , the folk symbol for property and inherited estate, today considered the equivalent of the rune *Odal*. This rune has also been found carved on trees in the New Forest together with **+** symbol, which is possibly a variation of the suncross mark,[256] a solar symbol that consists of an equal-armed cross within a circle which is later interpreted as a mark of consecration in churches.

---

256 Photo credit Simon Wood

I - ODAL & SUN CROSS ON A NEW FOREST TREE; PHOTO CREDIT SIMON WOOD

Another New Forest mark that must be mentioned in this chapter is the one depicted on the *Amberwood Stone*. Found in 1963 by Forestry workers, the Amberwood stone is a piece of sandstone about three inches across, which bears a raised symbol. The symbol itself is made of a type of mineral (hydrated iron-oxide limonite) which occurs naturally projecting from sandstone; however, the British Museum has described the shape of it as 'inconsistent with weathering'. This suggests that the stone may have been altered by human hand to create this symbol. According to Anthony Pasmore,[257] similar stones have been found in France and connections with witchcraft have been suggested. From some angles the symbol resembles the number 3, with an arrow shape at its head. However, I am inclined to turn the symbol round to see it from other angles, because it is all too easy for the eye to become committed to a familiar shape rather than consider other possible ones.

THE AMBERWOOD STONE, NOW IN THE RED HOUSE MUSEUM, CHRISTCHURCH

257 New Forest Pottery Kilns & Earthworks: Anthony Pasmore

St Mary's Church, Fordingbridge (12th century)

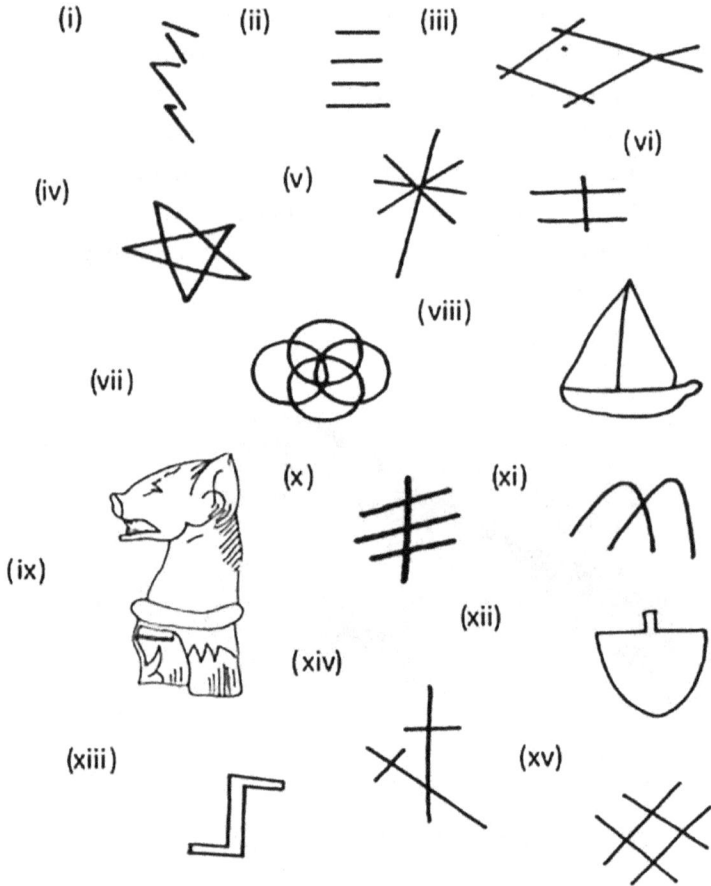

i.	LIGHTNING STRIKE
ii.	CONSECUTIVE LINES/'SPIRIT LADDER'
iii.	FISH
iv.	PENTAGRAM AT DOORWAY, SOUTH WALL
v.	8 SPOKED STAR
vi.	CONSECUTIVE LINES/'SPIRIT LADDER'
vii.	INTERSECTING CIRCLES AT DOORWAY, SOUTH WALL
viii.	BOAT/SHIP
ix.	DAEMON FACING NORTH WALL
x.	CONSECUTIVE LINES/'SPIRIT LADDER'
xi.	'MARION' CHARM
xii.	SHIELD
xiii.	POSSIBLE *EOH* ᛇ ('YEW/DEATH')
xiv.	CROSSED SWORDS
xv.	MESH SPIRIT TRAP/'LEGACY' CHARMS

The Royal Oak, Fritham (15th century)

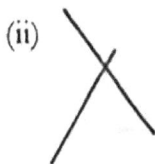

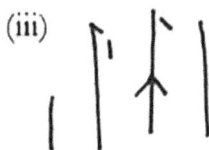

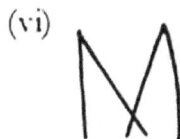

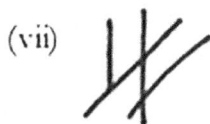

i.   'MARION' CHARM – OR DEER/CATTLE HOOF PRINT/KINGS MARK,
        WITH FOUR HOOF PRINTS/HORSESHOES
ii.   INCOMPLETE 'MARION' CHARM?
iii.   INCOMPLETE APOTROPAIC MARKS?
iv.   'MARION' CHARM
v.   POSSIBLE *NYD* ✝ ('NEED')
vi.   'MARION' CHARM
vii.   'MARION' CHARM
viii.   INCOMPLETE 'MARION' CHARM?

Waterditch Cottage, Poulner (17th century)

APOTROPAIC MARKS ON WINDOW MULLION

Woolpack Inn, Sopley (17th century)

APOTROPAIC MARKS ON CEILING BEAM
(TIMBER POSSIBLY REPURPOSED)

All Saints Church, Minstead (13th century)

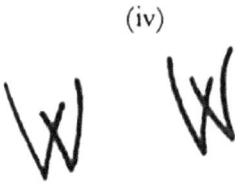

(i)   (ii)   (iii)

(iv)   (v)

i.	KINGS MARK
ii.	'MARION' CHARMS
iii.	MESH 'SPIRIT TRAP'
iv.	'MARION' CHARMS
v.	CONSECUTIVE LINES/'SPIRIT LADDER'

Verderers Court, Lyndhurst

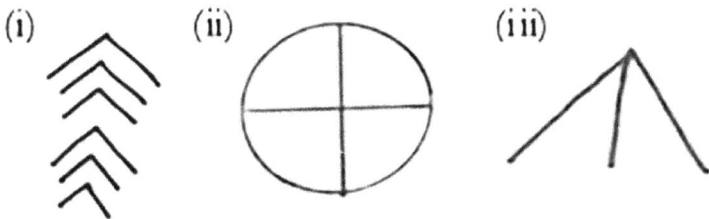

(i) **(ii)** **(iii)**

i.   CHEVRON ETCHINGS
ii. TARGET OR SUN CROSS
iii. KINGS MARK OR DEER HOOF

Queens House, Lyndhurst

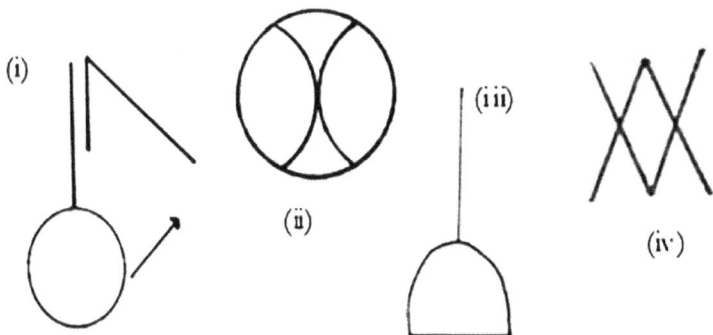

(i) **(ii)** **(iii)** **(iv)**

i.   EYELET/HOOK IMPRESSION MARKS
ii. INCOMPLETE HEXAFOIL
iii. STIRRUP
iv. LEGACY MARK

The Swan Pub, Lyndhurst

INCOMPLETE MARION MARKS?
ON WOODEN BEAM ABOVE FIREPLACE

St Marys, Carisbrooke, IOW

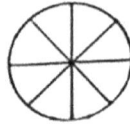

SUN WHEEL

Christchurch Priory, Christchurch

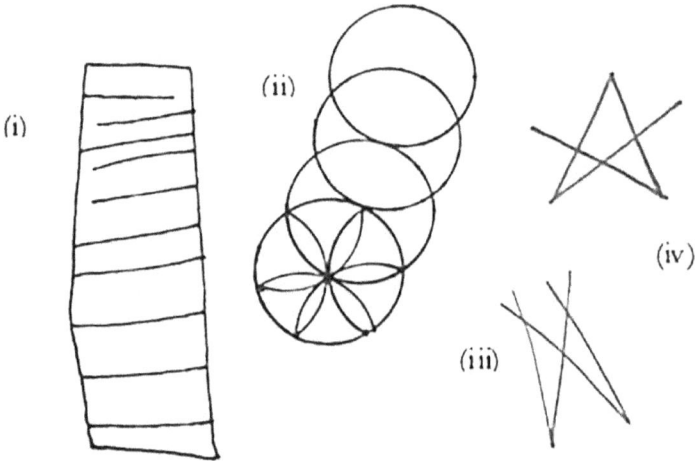

(i)

(ii)

(iii)

(iv)

i.	SPIRIT LADDER
ii.	CONSECUTIVE HEXAFOILS
iii.	MARION CHARM
iv.	INCOMPLETE PENTAGRAM

King John's House, Romsey

4 INTERSECTING DAISY WHEELS

Barn at Brightstone, IOW

BOAT OR SHIP

St Mary's, Eling

(i)   (ii)   (iii)

i.   LEGACY MARK
ii.   PENTAGRAM
iii.   MARION MARK

Various Tree Glyphs

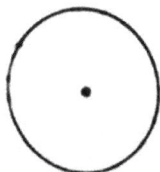  

INCOMPLETE HEXAFOILS & KINGS MARK

MIST ON THE MOORS: PLACES OF POWER

'The feeling of the people who live in the New Forest towards it, is something more than love; it is adoration, it is worship.'

H. Hutchinson: The New Forest

Within the boundaries of the New Forest are a wealth of intriguing places to visit; some are obvious whilst others remain subtle and hidden. Many of its most special places are largely forgotten, passed by in favour of the usual tourist attractions such as Boltons Bench or Burley High Street. Visitors rarely stray far from the car parks and in any case some of the most special places are only accessible by way of an hour or two's hike into the Forest, or by horse or bike. But for those who seek them out, the New Forest is full of exceptional places steeped in history and lore; places of power. This chapter gives just a snapshot of some which can be visited and is certainly not a complete list of all that the New Forest has to offer. The OS map can reveal lots of interesting features in the immediate area you are exploring, although many things are lost even to the modern OS maps. It is important to keep the memory of these places alive one way or another, and the old survey maps are a good place to start.

FORGOTTEN SACRED SPRINGS

Abbots Well & Spring, Frogham

This ancient dipping well was first recorded in 1215, although the natural spring that feeds the well is of course much older than even this. It emerges here on the plateau at Frogham, one of the highest points in the New Forest and is known for its ice-cold water that has *'the cold feel of the deep rock within it'*.[258] The ancient

---

258 Wanderers in the New Forest, Juliette de Bairacli Levy

settlement that would become today's village was built up around the well, which was still in use by the local community just a few generations ago, mains water only reaching the village as recently as 1951.[259] A local New Forest resident described to me how his great grandmother Daisy Witt and her husband Len (who lived in an old cottage on Abbots Well Road) used to collect their water from the well. It was also the main watering place for travellers along the old route to Southampton.[260] Moving towards Southampton along Hampton Ridge, the traveller would then have reached the village of Fritham where he could refresh himself at Irons Well (*Chalybeate*).

Like most wells and springs, Abbots Well would have been considered not only a practical source of water but also a sacred one, with cleansing and healing properties. The Abbots Well may have been considered particularly auspicious due to its vantage point over the Forest and Latchmore Brook beneath, which has its own rather sinister folklore (see *Latchmore*). There are also a number of tumuli (locally known as *butts*) in the surrounding Forest, indicating that this area was also anciently of spiritual importance. A boundary survey from 1215 mentions Abbots Well as a major landmark on the perambulation:

> *'upon Gorleydone (Gorley Hill) thence to Voxeslade (Foxholslade) and so across La Derrygge (Dorridge Hill) thence to Colinesford (near Ogdens) and so to (Ab)Biteswyle (Abbotts Well) thence to Gosley (Gawsley Bottom) and La Blisseford (Blissford)'.*

There are in fact two wells here. The main well is brick-lined with a wooden frame and lid, which can still be opened by a traveller. The other is a smaller uncovered well, presumably for animals to drink from, although Juliette de Bairacli Levy writes that the Romany children (who were so common in the area pre-1960's) used to collect water and wash their faces in the open pool.[261] It was also customary to submerge bee skeps (straw beehives) in the

---

259 With thanks to Ann Sevier, Chair of Hyde Parish Council & New Forest District Councillor
260 Hampshire Life, March 2017
261 Wanderers in the New Forest, Juliette de Bairacli Levy

Abbots Well each season in order to obtain the honey. The well is no longer regularly maintained, but on a good day water can still be gathered here. The well can be found at the very end of Abbotswell Road where it meets Hampton Ridge, the footpath which leads to Fritham, and is locally known as *Old Shutt.*[262] Both wells are framed by a fence made of traditional New Forest cleft-chestnut rails. According to local lore, another spring or well existed nearby which was known as *Caroline's Well* between here and Ogdens, although there is no evidence of this well on the 1789 Drivers Map, or on the track today. Also nearby, east of Godshill, is the *Geels Spring* or *Giles Well*, mentioned in ancient perambulations (boundary surveys) of the New Forest.

Picket Well, Hale

Picket Well is a fascinating water well with a very unusual, huge cone-shaped well cover, found just a few yards from the side of a steep narrow lane that winds its way through Hale village. The brick well itself dates from the 19th century, but the site appears on older maps as a natural spring and watering pool which had been used by the local community, travellers and for the horses of Hale Park House.[263]

The word *Picket* is a local New Forest term for something conical in shape such as a mound or a hill, but the name may also

ABBOTS WELL, FROGHAM – TWO DIPPING WELLS, ONE COVERED AND ONE OPEN FOR ANIMALS

---

262 Wanderers in the New Forest, Juliette de Bairacli Levy
263 Western Escarpment: NFPA Appraisal Document

have local connections to the New Forest Pixy Colt legend. As the locals tell it, the well must always be covered to prevent malign fairies from accessing the water, which might account for the strange, impenetrable shape of the well cover. Indeed, mounds (or butts) are themselves connected with the Pixy legend, and both connotations were probably seen as synonymous by the Hale residents. Old records describe how the spring was set in woodlands known locally over the years as both the *Osier Bed* (Osier: a term for a coppice of Willow trees) and the *Alder Moor*.[264] Both Willow and Alder are lovers of damp ground and grow near water. In the 1800's the woodland surrounding the well was ploughed and turned to crops, but just 30 years later was returned to its natural state - probably due to disapproval of the local fairies - and of course, the ground being far too wet to sensibly farm.

Lt Col. Gerald Goff, an amateur historian who inherited Hale Estate in 1871, gives accounts of how water divination was sometimes used to find water on the estate. He describes how a *'dividing rod man'* ... *'a water wizard'* named Mr A Berrow from Stalbridge visited Hale in 1888 to dowse at Home Farm. With the use of dowsing rods he divined that an underwater spring ran through in the field opposite Home Farm Cottages and explained that if they dug there, they would find water and that any well that built there would never dry up.[265] Water was indeed found about 13ft down, and it is rumoured that the well that was subsequently built there has never run dry. Incidentally, divining rods are also believed to be connected with the fairies who guide the rods, particularly to hoards and treasures.[266]

New Forest Chalybeate (iron-rich Wells and Springs)

Another well of particular interest is *Irons Well* or *Lepers Well* at Eyeworth near Fritham, a *chalybeate* well with water rich in iron and other curative minerals and a remedy used for a host of ailments such as sore eyes and arthritis. It runs red with iron salts, found as glutinous red deposits on its banks. The spring has been

264 History of Hale, Gerald L Goff
265 History of Hale, Gerald L Goff
266 The Forest in Folklore & Mythology: Alexander Porteous

known as *Irons Well* since at least 1789 as recorded on the Richardson, King & Drivers Map but given its properties, the likelihood is that the name will be considerably older than this. It was mostly known for its curative properties for leprosy, which was once widespread in Hampshire, but also to control mange in dogs. Today, this spring appears rather underwhelming, little more than a ditch stream that runs from beneath the earth and into the adjoining stream. This is one of those sites that you really have to 'be into this kind of thing' to appreciate. I took advantage of a good-natured friend to ride over to this spring and instructed him to scoop the red deposits up in his hand to 'tell me what it felt like' he wasn't impressed, but I was! However in 1893, Robert Charles Hope described the whole site quite differently:

> *'a little wooden structure over and round it, with a board wanting at the top, by which you may drop your dog into the chalybeate water; and a convenient arrangement exists by which, after he has finished his ablutions, he may scramble out on the other side.'* [267]

Fritham is a very old settlement with evidence of continued habitation, all likely to have built up around the water of the chalybeate spring and the ancient trackways which cross this point to other settlements. We find the first record of the village as *Frytham* in 1280 meaning *'scrub on the edge of a Forest'* and Eyeworth (the location of the well itself) possibly from *Luare* meaning *'streamside'* or *'marsh'*. There is evidence of prehistoric activity, and several Bronze Age barrows in the area. There are also examples of Roman pottery indicating its occupation and trading links. In the 19th century a gunpower factory was built at Fritham bringing a new sort of employment to the village. Unfortunately, the factory disposed of its chemical waste into the brook and caused considerable damage to marine life at that time and livestock refused to drink the water.[268] The pollution of the river continued right up until the 1920's when the factory was closed.

---

267 Legendary Lore of the Holy Wells in England: Robert Charles Hope
268 Discovering the New Forest: Sibley & Fletcher

Chalybeate springs are surprisingly common on the New Forest, due to the soil being rich in iron in many places. Another chalybeate spring known as *St Michael's Well* can be found just outside of Sopley. The structure around the well is a modern creation but built upon an ancient spring and given its chalybeate nature, this spring would also have been seen to offer both sacred and curative properties. It can be found on the opposite side of the road to the Woolpack Inn, on the gatepost of the entrance to The Old Clock House, just down the hill from the 13th century church St Michael's which itself was built on a tor-like mound and adjacent to the River Avon. Another also emerges in Burley, together with a dipping well named *Lady's Well*, or *Ladle Well*. The spring and well can be found down a glen which runs between properties; a natural run-off for water from higher ground into the stream below but also fed by several iron-rich springs. Like *Irons Well* at Fritham, these springs are abundant with viscous deposits of red iron salts, and the banks and low-lying trees along the glen are stained red with iron deposits. The well would benefit from some restoration as the banks surrounding the well have all but buried the frame, although some of the chestnut frame can still be seen. The brook below flows on towards the nearby Redrise Hill, a name which also promises of iron-rich water and soil. Iron springs can also be found emerging all along the New Forest cliff faces, such as at Milford on Sea and Hordle Cliffs.[269]

Tuttons Well, Christchurch

There are several other wells and springs across the New Forest, many of which once supported a settlement or activity but have now become hidden amongst the undergrowth or linger in obscure places, largely forgotten. However, one that has enjoyed a recent renovation is *Tuttons Well* (also previously recorded as *Putters Well* or *Tutters Well*)[270] in Stanpit, Christchurch; a freshwater spring which leads into the mouth of the nearby saltwater harbour. Accounts suggest *'the pure water is fed by underground springs,*

---

269 Geology of the New Forest: Ian West, Southampton University
270 The Legendary Lore of the Holy Wells of England, Robert Charles Hope

whose source is far inland, under the high hills of the New Forest.[271] Christchurch itself was held in special regard to its water; its Old English names Tweonea and Twinham-burn referring to its position between the River Avon and the River Stour.[272] An accompanying inscription claims that the site is Neolithic, probably correct considering its proximity to important sites nearby which reveal finds of human habitation as far back as the Palaeolithic era. This old dipping well was known for its exceptionally pure spring water, believed to cure many ailments but especially sore eyes[273] and even blindness, an ability which was utilised by the Monks at the nearby Christchurch Priory.[274] So effective were its abilities that according to an inscription at the site, the spring water was traded all around Britain as the *Christchurch Elixir* as an eyebath. There are records of the water being used for this purpose by local people as late as the 1930's.[275]

Originally a simple dipping well, at some stage a traditional-style structure was built around it complete with a roof and a bucket on a chain which was wound up and down with a handle, as recalled by a local born in the late 1800's.[276] At some point after this it was replaced with a stone surround and railings and much later overhauled in 2002, with a brand-new circular stone wall and a water pump with stone sink below. Today the well is chained closed, so it is impossible to draw water. However, another spring runs nearby just metres from the well, which is also commemorated by an inscription and runs incredibly clear. It is likely that the source of this spring is the same as the well, and the spring is probably the original sacred point of the site. I could easily have passed it by completely if not for a friend who said 'er, I think this is what we are really looking for!'

---

271 1933 Official Guide to Christchurch
272 John Richard de Capel Wise: The New Forest, Its History & Its Scenery
273 The Legendary Lore of the Holy Wells of England, Robert Charles Hope
274 Medical Aspects of Bournemouth and its Surroundings, Horace Dobell
275 The Christchurch Times, 21st July 1934
276 The Christchurch Times, 16th December 1958

Another New Forest spring known for curing eye disorders was *Kuckland Spring* (or *Buckland Spring*) in Lymington. Near Buckland Rings (a large Iron Age earthwork north of Lymington) this small spring was also reportedly held in high regard for generations for its medicinal properties.

Cursed Wells

I cannot finish this section of the book without mentioning the legendary Druid's Well on the Isle of Wight, which according to local lore once stood at the centre of the ancient oak forest where Brading Harbour is today. It was here that a druid imprisoned an evil water spirit inside the well, with the warning

TUTTONS WELL AT STANPIT, CHRISTCHURCH; SPRING WITH INSCRIPTION AND WELL

that anyone who should uncover the well would free the malign water spirit and be cursed. I don't think this was the inspiration for the 1998 horror *The Ring* but personally it's all I can think about when I hear this particular local legend!

STANDING STONES

Although rich in ancient boundary stones, unlike its neighbouring county Wiltshire Hampshire and the New Forest is sadly lacking in monoliths. However, although just outside of the Forest boundaries the Verwood Stone is close enough to make it onto our list. Found off the beaten track, this broad diamond-shaped fallen monolith is hidden amongst the bracken and gorse in a plantation of pine in Ringwood Forest, just north of Verwood. The sacred stone measuring a whopping 13ft long, 11.5ft wide and 2ft thick now lies flat but is believed to have once stood upright. The stone itself is Bagshot Bed gritstone, a quartz-rich deposit also used at Rempstone Circle near Corfe Castle.[277] The first written record of the stone was made in 1280, *'le Hoarstone near the road leading to the great bridge of Ringwood'* which refers to it as a boundary stone, or *bowerstone*.[278] After this the stone seems to have been largely forgotten until 1994, when local author Peter Knight together with the Verwood Historical Society managed to track down and excavate the monolith. The stone was named *Stephen's Stone* after the nearby iron age barrow called Stephen's Castle. As legend would have it, it was from here that an iron age tribal leader flung the three-tonne stone half a mile into the nearby Ringwood Forest, where it now lies. The assumption that the stone was simply a boundary marker has all but been abandoned since its rediscovery in 1994, with more contemporary knowledge pointing towards a ceremonial purpose. Its massive size and its shape alone - together with proximity to significant barrows - set it aside from a normal boundary marker. Either way, evidence has shown to me after two decades of visiting the site that the stone continues to be used for ritual purposes, having found burnt pages of the Bible and other such exciting discoveries there over the years.

There are also local legends of standing stones having once existed on the Isle of Wight, on Arreton Down and in the legendary ancient oak forest that Brading Harbour now occupies and that a henge of stones once stood at nearby Knowton, its stone broken up and rebuilt into the 12th century church. It is possible that the New Forest also had its own standing stone (or at least significant boundary stone) at Horestone Hill near Dibden Purlieu, the name *horestone* or *hoarstone* usually suggesting a stone of some presence. The site is recorded in the 1670 perambulation, *'Horestone Hill, anciently Strayhup'* whilst across the water on the Isle of Wight, the *Longstone* stands at the village of Mottistone, a ritual meeting stone or 'moot stone' that was flung there by the devil and left its legacy in the name of the village.[279] We find other

---

277 Ancient Stones of Dorset, Peter Knight
278 John Richard de Capel Wise: The New Forest, Its History & Its Scenery
279 The Folklore of Hampshire and the Isle of Wight: Wendy Boase

reminders of the devil making his mark on the land; such as *Divells Den* near Blackwater (mentioned in the 1670 perambulation) and Rollstone Lane (now Rollestone Road) in the same area which gives some tentative suggestions to stones being shifted by daemons and land spirits. Other stones in the area are also believed to have been moved from place to place by supernatural means. According to legend, Christchurch Priory was originally supposed to be built on the top of St Catherine's Hill, but the stones that were taken up to the hill by day would reappear back in the valley below overnight, allegedly moved by diabolical hands.[280]

Giants, too, are blamed for moving stones around for fun. A local giant named *Onion* was responsible for the 'imp stone' which stands on the border of Hampshire and Berkshire, after allegedly hurling it from Silchester.[281] Giants are a popular motif within Hampshire legend, such as a giant who ate children at Blackgang Chine, a coastal ravine on the Isle of Wight - a ghoulish bedtime story which explained the reddish water that ran down the cliff face.[282]

MIGHTY TREES & GALLOW POSTS OF THE NEW FOREST

As one might expect, the trees of the Forest are an important part of this landscape with both acres of ancient woodlands and a number of trees which are considered as particularly notable. One such place is the site of an old oak tree which stands at the centre of New Forest lore. Marked on the OS map as the *Naked Man* (but often referred to by local people as the *Wilverley Oak*) the original tree has all but gone, having been struck by lightning several times and reduced to a stump. However, another oak tree was planted at the site some 15 years ago and this continues to thrive, protected by traditionally cut New Forest cleft-chestnut rails. The site of the tree stands on Wilverley Plain near the crossroads known as Wilverley Post, where the road between

---

280 John Richard de Capel Wise: The New Forest, Its History & Its Scenery
281 The Folklore of Hampshire and the Isle of Wight: Wendy Boase
282 The Folklore of Hampshire and the Isle of Wight: Wendy Boase

Christchurch and Lyndhurst (now the A31) meets the old route between Sway and Burley. The part of the route that ran past the Naked Man was at one time made suitable for vehicles but has now been returned to the Forest as a footpath. Either way, the route has always been an important and ancient byway and even a link to the train station at Holmsley when the old railway still ran, just on the other side of Wilverley inclosure. The site is recorded as far back as 18th century, also marked as the *Naked Man* on the 1789 Drivers map.

As folk history would have it, as seen from the eastern side, the battered old tree once resembled a naked man, and this is how it got its name; described in 1924 by the historian Heywood Sumner as '*a trunk with two arms...its spine wood even now repels a knife.*' However other lore describes how the tree was used for hanging highway men, a gallow tree (in other parts of the British Isles, a 'grief tree')[283] and that the name developed from the sight of stripped criminals swaying from its boughs. Indeed, several hanging points are rumoured to have existed in the New Forest. A New Forest hanging post is said to have stood on the village green at Sway. Local legend has it that a 'Mr Samuel Way' (S.WAY) is said to have been hung here for smuggling and so the village got its name (however, the word Sway actually comes from the Old English *Svieia*, 'noisy stream' or *Swaeth*, meaning 'a track through the Forest' or possibly even the Old English for 'sow enclosure').[284] There was also allegedly a gallows at the cheerfully named Deadman's Hill near Fordingbridge, and Hutchinson writes that the last Englishman to be hung by chains was executed at Bramshaw, a criminal who robbed an elderly woman and set fire to her house.[285] At Breamore we find Gallows Hill, an old hanging site and the location of a number of round barrows. This gallow site is also not far from *Grim's Ditch* (said to have been

283 The Forest in Folklore & Mythology: Alexander Porteous
284 The New Forest Historical Landscape: Sue Davies, Karen Walker & Linda Coleman
285 The New Forest, Its Traditions, Inhabitants and Customs: De Crespigney & H Hutchinson

carved from the earth by the devil) and the *Giant's Grave Long Barrow*. A rather interesting and macabre area of the Downs.

It is worth considering the links of hanging trees to occult learning. One is reminded of the Norse god Woden *'Lord of Gallows'*[286] who was stripped of all material belongings and hung from a tree for 9 days and nights, to divine the meaning of the runes in a pool of water beneath him, a legend which is particularly poignant given the links of the Jutish people who once lived here and brought the cult of Woden to our shores. Woden also became identified and conflated with the old deities and land spirits of the British Isles. Indeed, the Naked Man has been important to the resurgence of the esoteric in Britain with several influential individuals using the site since at least the 1930's including Doreen Valiente, Sybil Leek and from further afield, Janet Farrar. The author and occultist Gerald Gardner, a resident of the New Forest village of Highcliffe also used this site and its surrounding moors. Most famously, the site is a possible location for Gardner's *Operation Cone of Power*, several rituals carried out by Gardner and other members of the New Forest Coven in 1940 to stop the Germans from crossing the sea (another site was possibly Hengistbury Head or the mouth of Chewton Bunny). It is rumoured that the rituals were so intense that several people fell sick and even died from exhaustion and exposure. But evidently the magic worked, the Germans did not cross into England. The Naked Man has also become the resting place for the ashes of a number of influential people, some renowned and other more private individuals. This book does not cover the New Forest's involvement in this topic much further but please refer to Philip Heselton's fabulous book *'In search of the New Forest Coven'*.

At Moyles Court in Rockford there stand several fabulous and ancient oak trees. To the casual observer these are nothing more than wayside oaks, however when considering the geography and history of the local area the importance of these trees becomes clear. The crossroads of Moyles Court offers four directions –

---

286 The Forest in Folklore & Mythology: Alexander Porteous

Linwood to the east, the old road to Linford Bottom to the south, Ringwood to the west and Ibsley to the north, where it crosses the stream *Dockens Water* (Dockens meaning 'dark', 'secluded'). This meeting place between old trackways and Dockens Water was important to our ancestors and even leaves its legacy in its name; Rockford being from the Old English *Rooks Ford* ('Rooks Ford over Dockens Water').[287] It is clear that this particular New Forest crossroad has always been an important place. The Moyles Court manor house (now a private independent school) was first built in the Reign of Charles II[288] on the site of another stately residence and is likely to have been an important site to settlers much earlier this. There is evidence of some 4000 years of habitation of the Moyles Court area as artefacts found here and at the nearby Rockford Common prove[289] and Rockford was a flourishing area with its own little school right up until the 1960's. The lack of young local children caused the school to close, and the school building is now the *Alice Lisle* pub. It is probably true to say that the increasing monetary value of properties in the New Forest has pushed many young families out. At one time properties were built on the Forest to provide poorer local families with a home, now those properties are worth millions and so many bought by retired city-dwellers or holiday homes for the rich. With this, we have lost a great deal of New Forest common folk tradition.

Back to the trees. One of the oaks, which stands in a prominent position at the crossroads in a north-easterly position is particularly old and even marked on the OS map (simply as 'Oak'). The tree is estimated to be at least 600 years old, so was already growing in the 1400's. Writing in 1921, Heywood Sumner recorded the girth of the tree at a massive 19ft and 8 inches, well over a foot longer than the measurement taken by Wise just 60 years earlier.[290] The tree has suffered in more recent years,

287 The New Forest Historical Landscape: Sue Davies, Karen Walker & Linda Coleman
288 The New Forest, Heywood Sumner
289 The New Forest, Heywood Sumner
290 The New Forest, Heywood Sumner

probably not only due to its sheer age but also the encroachment of the tarmac road and increased traffic, both vehicular and pedestrian which has compacted the surrounding soil. However, when last recorded in the 1990's the girth is now around 22ft[291] so despite appearances, the tree is still enduring! Opposite the main tree in a south-westerly direction stands another mighty oak; slightly smaller and of a lesser age, hollowed and obscured by hedges, but ancient still. Looking between these two trees creates an avenue of vision in the south-east and with water-splash behind us in the north, we find evidence of the ancient settlements and encampments, including bee gardens and livestock enclosures, burn mounds and earthworks, including tumuli and iron age banks and pillow mounds. It is believed that many more earthworks would have existed but have since been destroyed when the area was excavated for gravel. There are spectacular views across the Forest from the Rockford Common bowl barrow and on a clear day, sitting on the barrow eating fish and chips, we have been able to see right across Blashford Lakes, the Avon Valley and even as far as the Purbecks.

The Rockford Oak is considered one of the oldest trees in the New Forest, only contending with the perhaps better-known Knightwood Oak referred to as the *'Queen of the Forest'*. Last recorded with a 24ft girth, the Knightwood Oak can be found on Rhinefield Ornamental Drive, between Christchurch and Lyndhurst. Another tree worth mentioning for its size is the Spreading Oak, which is also marked on the OS map not far from Ocknell inclosure and has a girth of around 19ft. A tree of true legendary notoriety was the Cadnam Oak, which once stood at a crossroads in the village of Cadnam (around grid reference SU292136). According to folklore, the Cadnam Oak bloomed with buds and green leaves during mid-winter (or by other accounts, only on Christmas Eve or Old Christmas Night)[292] while all other trees remained leafless and barren. Just over a mile away, the Rufus Oak which allegedly deflected the arrow that

---

291 New Forest Explorers Guide website
292 John Richard de Capel Wise: The New Forest, Its History & Its Scenery

killed William II or William 'Rufus' ('Red') in 1100 (although other locations are also suggested) also displayed this miraculous blooming during mid-winter.

Whilst excessively touristy in the summer months, the Redwoods are also worth a visit. Although not native to the Forest, the pair of Redwoods were planted in the 1800's and are now a spectacular feature of the local landscape, creating an otherworldly gateway into the woodlands beyond. The trees can be found just across the road from the Blackwater Arboretum car park, Rhinefield Ornamental Drive, close to the A35 between Christchurch and Lyndhurst. The site is best visited during the winter or mid-week as it is more peaceful outside of peak times! It is particularly interesting at night, although parking is not permitted at night in the Forest.

> *'Moss and lichen ... clothe trunks and limbs, while butchers broom and strange toadstools grow in the crotches of the roots. These old woods hold the spell of magic.'*
>
> The Ancient Earthworks of the New Forest,
> Heywood Sumner

The trees of the New Forest are also known for their association with otherworldly spirits. Across the British Isles and beyond there is a common motif that the *genii* (protective spirit of place) lives within the oldest tree on the landscape known as the *King of the Forest.* For obvious reasons, it is considered very unlucky to cut this tree down.[293] The trickster spirit Puck or Pooka is known to particularly enjoy frolicking under the boughs of ancient oak trees, whilst it is possible to see otherworldly spirits by gazing through a *'tree hole'* in an old crab-apple (much like a hag-stone). Other spirits are known to dwell beneath the roots of ancient trees. *Imp trees* are also known for their connection with fairies, an anomaly where two trees have naturally grown together.[294] The Rockford Oak has earned himself the name of *Woodman* with local children. Woodman is a giant who disguises as a tree when any observer looks at him; his feet are rooted into the

---

293 The Forest in Folklore & Mythology: Alexander Porteous
294 The Forest in Folklore & Mythology: Alexander Porteous

ground and he watches all who pass by. Should you gaze at him, he will camouflage himself by closing his eyes - but only just, so he can still watch you. This local giant sounds almost as ominous as the *ash-ogre*, which in some parts of the British Isles is known to inhabit ash trees.[295]

KNOWLTON HENGE

Knowlton Henge is an amazing place in the village of Knowlton, near Wimborne, just to the west of the New Forest. Although it stands outside of the Forest boundaries, there is no doubt that it was a significant site both known to and used by those dwelling in and around the New Forest. As archaeologist Nicholas Thomas suggests, Knowlton was probably 'akin to Stonehenge' in the late Neolithic and the early Bronze Age.[296] The main central henge is approximately 350ft x 310ft and probably once held great stone megaliths, in a similar style to Stonehenge. Its internal ditches indicate that this site was certainly ceremonial rather than defensive and would have been used ceremonially around 2500-1700 BCE. The stones are no longer there but it is generally thought that the stones were reworked into the foundations of the 12th century church (with 15th century additions) which now stands at the centre of the henge. There is also another huge earthwork nearby, described as the 'south circle' with an 800ft diameter, but this is now bisected by a road. Another smaller circle stands in the north, and a huge number of tumuli surrounding the site with barrow cemeteries both to the north and south of the main site. One barrow that is closer to the main central henge is the largest known barrow in Dorset, measuring 20ft high x 135ft diameter.

Knowlton remains an important spiritual centre in the area. It is somewhat of a 'marmite' place, there is a subtle yet powerful energy which lies just beneath the surface, which some people enjoy and others dislike. Two sacred yew trees just outside of the henge have become *clootie trees*, a place to make offerings or

---

295 The Forest in Folklore & Mythology: Alexander Porteous
296 Ancient Stones of Dorset: Peter Knight

wishes. Anyone leaving an offering should bear in mind whether their offering is biodegradable or not. Last time I visited the site, I had to untie a number of pieces of plastic carrier bags that had been tied to the tree! A most bizarre offering - please don't forget also that most ribbons contain plastic. Instead, my son made a spiral out of the tiny white stones which are plentiful on the site; that was a better idea.

GREAT WITCH & LITTLE WITCH

These twin hillocks can be found next to Haseley inclosure, overlooking Latchmore near Ogdens and are natural formations known as 'twin spurs'. They are named *Great Wytch* and *Little Wytch* on the 1789 Drivers Map but it's likely the names are much older than this. I was obviously very keen to find out the origin of their names especially as this site is in walking distance from my home, a somewhat syncretic moment when I spotted them on the map. It is not known how they got their intriguing names, but as with some other natural formations in the area, they may have once been considered as barrows and therefore seen as having otherworldly, liminal properties. Otherwise, the word 'witch' is linked to *wych* which can mean 'brine spring'. Whilst no brine springs are known in the area today, inland acidic springs can occur inland in the New Forest[297] therefore its theoretically possible that springs with unusual types of water were all at one time referred to as wych springs. The word is also linked to elms (the wych elm). Elms are associated with death, their wood being used for coffins; the tree is also associated with prophetic dreams.[298] These two hillocks also have some interesting wartime history. The surrounding area was under the control of the military during WW2 (Ashley Walk bombing range) and an eyewitness remembers a 20ft trench being dug into Great Witch and used to detonate unexploded bombs against.[299]

---

297 With thanks to Ian West, Southampton University
298 The Woodland Trust website – Wych Elm
299 *New Forest Notes*, April 2010 – www.newforesthistoryandarchaeology.co.uk

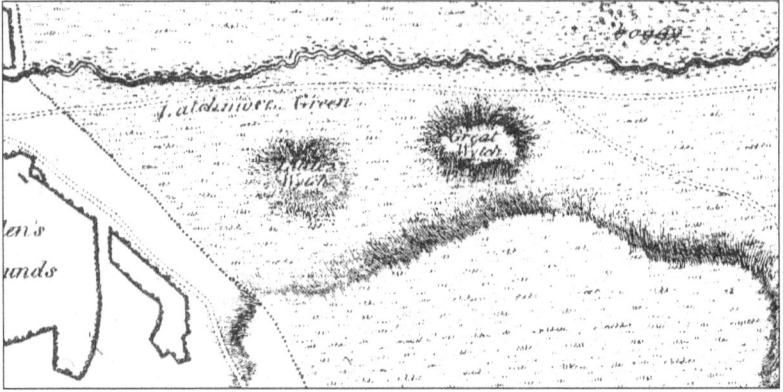

GREAT WITCH AND LITTLE WITCH, 1789 DRIVERS MAP

LIMINAL PLACES

Into the Forest I go
To lose my mind and find my soul.

The Hiking Notebook: John Muir

Sinking Mud: Morass & Mire

The bogs of the New Forest are truly infamous, rumoured to swallow both walker and beast if given half the chance; after a hunt in 1637, King Charles was so displeased by the weather and the boggy ground he demanded that bridges and causeways be installed before his next visit![300] Significant tracts of bog are marked on Forest maps as *morass* or *mire*, and many place names in the Forest include the word *more, moor* or *moore* in their name meaning *'area of marsh'*. Part of the reason why the New Forest has retained its wilderness is the makeup of the ground and soil, which generally consists of sand and gravel topsoil with clay beneath. Any rainwater washes straight off the topsoil and down into lower areas, where it sits on the clay and as a result, much of the low-lying ground is boggy and damp. Luckily perhaps, as this makes a large proportion of the Forest unsuitable for building upon and provides ecosystems for a host of wetland birds and aquatic creatures. Scarce plants also thrive here, including bogbean, sundew, coral necklace, pennywort, bog pimpernel and

---

300 A History of Hunting in Hampshire: Brig. Gen. JFR Hope

bog asphodel. Many of the bogs are great carpets of yellow-brown moss and aromatic bog myrtle, sprigs of which can be tied together and hung in the house, as local lore says it keeps the flies away. On higher ground we find green-grey lichen, which indicates only the purest air, and polypody fern and fungi growing amongst the tree roots.

Bogs are also often indications of underground water springs, pure water bubbling up out of the ground enriched with minerals. The wettest ground is usually found in the lowland valleys of the Forest (locally known as *'bottoms'*) with the giveaway white-tufted flowers of the cottongrass. A local proverb warns not to ride where the white flowers bloom! Other bogs are encountered in unexpected places, such as on the very top of wind-beaten, dry hilltops just metres away from main tracks and solid ground. In other cases, the bogs are sinister-looking patches of black ooze, with an appearance like petrol, which dries and cracks in the summer but, lethally, remains wet underneath. Walkers will often try to cross bogs to shorten their journey, whilst a local will be seen taking the longer route round! New Forest children refer to the bogs as *sinking mud* and develop a respect for the morass at an early age. By the age of 3, my son had already grasped a knowledge of the wet ground and by five, could safely cross the bogland behind our house with (hardly!) any help.

The bogs play a big part in the folklore of the New Forest. Wet ground can be a particular danger when crossing unfamiliar moors and is known to be haunted by the *Colt Pixy*, a local trickster spirit that entices travellers into the bogs. A similar legend exists in Worcestershire, involving the trickster spirit *Poake* (Puck) who leads unsuspecting travellers to their demise. Once they are thoroughly stuck, he *'sets up a loud laugh and leaves them quite bewildered in the lurch*[301] and the traveller is said to have been *poake-ledden*. The Colt Pixy folklore appears to be particularly prevalent surrounding tumuli found on high ground overlooking bogs and damp valleys.

---

301 J. Allies: On the Ignis Fatuus

Will-o'-the-Wisp

These foolish fires, giving more light than heat.

- Shakespeare's Hamlet

Because of their notorious reputation, the bogs have found their own place at the heart of New Forest folklore. Generally considered the enemy of the traveller, the bogs are believed to be the territory of several malign spirits whose single purpose is to lure the unsuspecting into the bogs of the New Forest, delaying a journey or worse, sending the traveller to an untimely demise. The *Will-o'-the-Wisp* (or *ignis fatuus*, Latin for *'foolish fire'*) is one such Forest spirit seen on the moors and believed to entice people towards the mire by impersonating a lamp; at first glance, a welcomed sight to a lost or disorientated traveller in the night. This effervescent pixie-light is often described as a fine, blue-white flame that draws a traveller towards it but then either becomes intensely bright or suddenly extinguishes, causing them to blunder into a bog.[302] Not limited to the New Forest, the *Will-o'-the-Wisp* is perhaps one of the more well-known bog-dwelling

---

302 Wirt Sikes: British Goblins

apparitions. There is a superstition also familiar to much of the British Isles that should one find themselves lost as a result of being *poake-ledden* or *pixy-led* you can escape the faeries' grasp by turning a piece of clothing (such as a coat or glove) inside out.[303] If not done soon enough, you might find yourself drawn into a mire.

> *Are you not he,*
> *That frights the maidens of the village,*
> *Misleads night-wanderers, laughing at their harm?*

Shakespeare's Midsummer-Nights Dream

The pixie *William* is believed to carry the 'Wisp' of light (i.e., 'Will with a Wisp') a 'wisp' being in the appearance of a twist of straw. Will is also personified as the spirit *Jack* (Jack-o-Lantern) or *Puck (Pwca/Pooka)* who Shakespeare describes as transforming into fire. In the New Forest where legends of Puck are plentiful, it is likely that the wisp spirit was considered another manifestation of the *Pooka*. DE Jenkins writes in Bedd Gelert: Its Facts, Fairies & Folklore, *'people say his laugh was not unlike the loud sudden neighing of a horse.'* The connection to the local trickster spirit the Collepixie is also clear, also enticing the unsuspecting traveller into treacherous bogs. Some say that the Will-o'-the-Wisp and Puck are agents of the Collepixie itself. In the New Forest, the wisp is also sometimes referred to as the *Glowblow* - quite a mouthful, but descriptive, nonetheless! Some local placenames possibly make reference to this phenomenon due to their proximity to regular Will-o'-the' Wisp apparitions. The phenomenon is explained by science as a type of bioluminescence, caused by organic decay which releases a flammable gas and creates a flashing glow above the bog when it reaches oxygen.

---

303 Traditional Witchcraft, A Cornish Book of Ways: Gemma Gary

Lakes & Ponds, Streams & Beaches

Below my casement wide, a little stream
Murmurs and ripples in a happy dream
Winding its way around each moss-grown tree
Threading its fairy path to the sea.

Dorothy Clutterbuck,
writing at her home in Mill House, Walkford 1927

Not limited to bogs and damp low-lying valleys, liminality can also be found in other places where water meets land in the Forest such as lakes, ponds, streams, saltmarshes and beaches. The shores of the New Forest are possibly some of the most unique in the land, where in some places the cattle, donkeys and ponies can roam freely on the beach grazing on seaweeds and grasses. The ocean itself can be strangely atmospheric offshore from the New Forest, as John Richard de Capel Wise wrote in the late 1800's of the effects that can be seen at Barton on Sea,

Far out at sea will rise a low white fog-bank, gradually
stealing to the land ... encircling the Island, whilst the chalk
cliffs melt into clouds. On it steals with its thick mist,
quenching the Needles' light ...until neither sea nor sky can
be seen ... Then suddenly the wind lifts the cloud ...
revealing a sky of the deepest blue ... the whole bay suddenly
shines out clear and glittering the Island cliffs flashing with
opal and emerald. [304]

We also find the salterns which were used for salt production, an industry which thrived at Eling, Dibden, Hordle and Lymington right up until the 19th century.

Chewton Bunny & the Modern Witchcraft Movement

Keystone under the hearth,
keystone under the horse's belly.

New Forest Proverb

Gradually moving inland, we find more waterside places wrapped up in local history and folklore. In the New Forest, a gully or glen (which is formed by a stream running down to the

---

304 John Richard de Capel Wise: The New Forest, Its History & Its Scenery

sea) is called a *bunny*. One such Glen is *Chewton Bunny* at Walkford, in Highcliffe, which follows the Walkford Brook to the sea.[305] Already immersed in local history, Chewton Bunny had been a regular landing place and route into the New Forest for smugglers as early as the 13th century. These secluded landing places joined up to a number of trafficking routes that were used across the Forest, sunken tracks worn by travellers which led to trading places such as Smugglers Road between Burley and Crow; Wise writes that smuggled goods were then hidden either under the fireplace or under the stable floor.[306]

But in the 1900's Chewton Bunny would enter the history books again for a very different reason, when it became a nucleus of the modern witchcraft movement. It was here on Mill Lane (which leads into the Chewton Bunny footpath) that Dorothy Clutterbuck (1880-1951) would write about the fairies and nature spirits that inhabited Walkford Brook; she also wrote a number of goddess and nature-focused poems throughout the 1900's.[307] Dorothy was a wealthy woman from an upper-class family, known for her charitable work. One of her closest friends, Katherine Oldmeadow (1878-1963) lived just a stone's throw from Chewton Bunny in *The Glen House* on the corner of Mill Lane. Katherine was also an affluent woman of means who wrote a number of books - fiction, non-fiction and poetry all reflecting an interest in divination, initiation and magic (before anything of the sort was freely available on the bookshelves). Like Dorothy Clutterbuck, Katherine also had a connection with the nature spirits at Chewton Bunny and a love for other 'pagan' themes surrounding the natural environment of this area of the New Forest. Ian Stevenson wrote how she absolutely believed in fairies and *'undoubtably regarded Chewton Glen as a magical place.*[308] Katherine Oldmeadow also had several Romany friends, particularly from the area of Thorney Hill who she claimed supplied her with a wealth of folk knowledge and cures, many of which made their

---

305 In the nearby Bournemouth area, it is called a *Chine*.
306 John Richard de Capel Wise: The New Forest, Its History & Its Scenery
307 Philip Heselton: Wiccan Roots
308 Gurth Brooke interview with Ian Stevenson, 2005

way into her book *The Folklore of Herbs,* published in 1946.[309] It is probably worthwhile mentioning here, a little piece of history that may give some insight into why these affluent women from Highcliffe became involved with the Gypsy women of the New Forest. Len Smith writes in his book *Romany Nevi-Wesh* that it was common for wealthy local philanthropic ladies to be involved in charity work for the New Forest Gypsies, especially related to the Romany women such as funding for and often providing such things as wedding rings, wedding dresses and jewellery. Certainly, to assist the Gypsy families in this way would earn their favour and it is my suspicion that both women were involved in supporting the local Gypsy community. In return, they received information relating to herbal lore, superstitions and fortune-telling.

As with the Gypsy community, both women also had connections with local practitioners of witchcraft and perhaps practised themselves. The area of Highcliffe and Christchurch was a melting pot for individuals and organisations supporting spiritual and occult study and they were all moving in the same circles. Specifically, Clutterbuck and Oldmeadow would have come to know two women named Rosamund Sabine and Edith Woodford-Grimes. Both lived in the Highcliffe area and known to have had links to other local practitioners of witchcraft from the region, such as the Mason family of Southampton and other local working-class people who 'held old knowledge'.[310] Clutterbuck and Oldmeadow were involved at the very least in a supportive capacity. Dorothy allowed practitioners of witchcraft to use her property in Mill Lane (*The Mill House*) to conduct their meetings and rituals. The jury is still out as to whether Dorothy was actually a member of the coven herself, but several accounts like to imply she was in fact a position of authority - possibly even the High Priestess. She is said to have 'called up the covens' to unite for the Operation Cone of Power in 1940.[311] Gerald

---

309 The Christchurch Times, 12th July 1963
310 Philip Heselton: In Search of the New Forest Coven
311 Jack Bracelin: Gerald Gardner, Witch

Gardner's initiation into witchcraft in 1939 was held either here at The Mill House or possibly on the grounds of her other property *Latimers*, in Hinton Wood Avenue, also in Highcliffe. *'Gardner...was taken to a big house in the neighbourhood. This belonged to Old Dorothy ... It was in this house that he was initiated into witchcraft.*[312] As Gerald Gardner recounts, *'Old Dorothy, and a number of New Forest people, had kept the light shining.'*[313] Katherine's sister Ann may also have been involved. See Philip Heselton's excellent books, *Wiccan Roots* and *In Search of the New Forest Coven*, for more on this topic.

Watercourses as Landmarks & Places of Legend

John Wise wrote in the 1800's how the ancient Britons left traces of their rule in the names of the rivers we know today and gives ancient meanings, such as the River Exe (*wysg* - 'the current') the River Avon (*afon* - 'the river') and the River Stour (*wys-dwr* - 'deep water').[314] Our ancestors were relied upon the rivers for transport and particularly fishing; fish were plentiful in our local rivers and the River Avon is said to have contained more fish species than any other river in Britain.[315] The watercourses were also important to our ancestors geographically, with the earliest 'perambulations' (boundary surveys) appearing to be defined largely by topographic features such as rivers and setting a prescient for future boundaries.[316] For instance, the limits of the Forest during the reign of William I defined the boundaries as extending to the River Avon on the west, the sea to the south and the River Blackwater to the east.[317] Key towns and villages on-route of the rivers came to be included such as Christchurch, Fordingbridge and Ringwood and Forest extremities were known to reach as far north-easterly as *Owerbridge* (Ower) and as far west

312 Jack Bracelin: Gerald Gardner, Witch
313 Gardner recounting to Jack Bracelin: Gerald Gardner, Witch
314 John Richard de Capel Wise: The New Forest, Its History & Its Scenery
315 New Forest Commoner (Blog) www.newforestcommoner.co.uk
316 The New Forest Historical Landscape: Sue Davies, Karen Walker & Linda Coleman
317 The New Forest Historical Landscape: Sue Davies, Karen Walker & Linda Coleman

as Charford, near Downton.[318] The boundaries were later formalised and curtailed and all of these places are now outside the official Forest boundaries.

The watercourses of the New Forest have some folklore about them too. One of the most infamous local river legends surrounds Latchmore Brook, which runs through Latchmore Bottom towards Gorley from the Fritham direction. The word Latchmore has two different origins which have become conflated in the mists of time; one from *Laece, Lache, Latch,* Old English for '*a stream through a bog*'[319] and others from *Litch* or *Lych* meaning 'leech pool' or 'dead body, corpse'. On older maps, Latchmore was often spelled as 'Litchmore' and as such, locally Latchmore is known as the '*marsh of corpses*'. There were many tumuli in the area, some which have now been levelled and it may be that this area was historically known to be associated with the dead, hence being gifted the name of Latchmore. Local legend has it that in some distant past a great battle was fought at Latchmore Bottom and the bodies were piled up in Latchmore Brook; Juliette de Bairacli Levy writes that skeletons were found there.[320] Latchmore has another association with floating bodies. In the late 1800's a gunpowder factory was built at Eyeworth near Fritham and a dam was built to create a reservoir (now known as Eyeworth Pond). Unfortunately, the factory disposed of its chemical waste into the brook and caused a mass-death of fish and other marine life and dead fish were seen floating down the stream for years, truly a marsh of corpses. This continued right up until the 1920's, when the factory closed. This whole area was also used as bombing practice during the Second World War (Ashley Walk Bombing Range). There are exciting remnants of WW2 all along Hampton Ridge, including a bomber target arrow and a bunker, which after the war was covered up with soil rather than destroyed and now resembles a barrow. It is probably only hearsay that fallen planes and unexploded bombs are sunken into

---

318 H. Hutchinson: The New Forest
319 The New Forest: Heywood Sumner
320 Wanderers in the New Forest, Juliette de Bairacli Levy

the bogs below Hampton Ridge; although live bombs were dropped in the area and one plane did crash here in 1943. However, even today there are accounts of the sound of exploding bombs being carried on the air across the valley at night.

There also used to be a Latchmore Pond with similar associations just outside of Brockenhurst which again, the author John R Wise accounts of being known locally as the *'pond of corpses'*[321] almost certainly due to its proximity to a number of barrows nearby on Setley Plain (in particular rare twin disc barrows). The pond is marked on the 1789 Drivers Map and remembered today in local names of Latchmoor House and Latchmoor Farm, however the pond no longer exists. It's likely that the pond was drained when the rail line was built; the Lymington River which would have fed the pond still passes by here.

Another place of interest are the banks of the River Stour near Throop Mill, a traditional watermill which lies just outside of the boundaries of the New Forest. A Mill has stood on the site since at least the 11th century and is mentioned in the Domesday Book. The Stour was known in times gone by for its crystal-clear water, a haven for wildlife and fishing, although sadly it seems both are now suffering here. The ford which bridges the Stour, just a short distance downstream from the Mill, is mentioned in the legends of Sir Walter Tirel who crossed this Ford as he fled the scene of the murder of William II or William 'Rufus' ('Red') slain in 1100.

> *The blow of Gods vengeance is bent against the wicked.*
> *The arrow, swift to wound, is already drawn out of the*
> *quiver. Soon will the blow be struck...* [322]

Some unusual accounts have also been made of the riverbanks near the Mill, such as a woman's voice whispering the names of walkers and fishermen near the waters' edge. A friend and I experienced this when I was about 17 and before I was aware of any of the history of the site. There is a phenomenon known as

---

321 John Richard de Capel Wise: The New Forest, Its History & Its Scenery
322 Fulchered, Abbot of Shrewsbury

the *voice-folk* - disembodied voices that lure you towards them, your fate to be spirited away to become one of them.[323] The Mill itself also has some suspicion surrounding it. After the Mill's closure in 1970's, several projects have been started to renovate the building into a heritage centre, café or housing but all projects have so far failed, with the Mill falling further into disrepair. It is somewhat plagued by sinister stories of dark figures who pace the Mill, and the sound of children playing and crying inside the Mill at night. Local folklore says that in the 1800's several children went missing from the village, perhaps lost in the waters behind the Mill.

Mist Ponds & Bottomless Lakes

The New Forest also has a number of ponds, both natural and man-made, either natural formations or a result of human intervention (such as excavation for gravel/clay/marl and even old bomb-craters, such as *Tallboy Crater* near Pitts Wood inclosure) which are a haven for birds and aquatic life, many decorated with beautiful pond plants, such as the flowering waterlily ponds at East End near Norleywood and Eyesworth near Fritham.

Many of these ponds in the New Forest are known as *Mist Ponds* or *Dew Ponds*; temporary ponds which remain dry during the summer but fill up during rainfall. They are watering opportunities for stock but also a vital breeding ground for wildlife such as small amphibians, crustaceans and insects, which would otherwise be preyed upon by fish in permanent ponds and rivers. In many dew ponds in the New Forest, research[324] has found the rare crustacean known as the *Fairy Shrimp (Chirocephalus diaphanous)* which thrives from the bottom of the water being disturbed by drinking/wading animals[325] the perfect symbiotic relationship in an environment where stock roam freely. Another ancient Mist Pond is Ocknell Pond, near Stoney Cross. Already

---

323 The Forest in Folklore & Mythology: Alexander Porteous
324 New Forest Fairy Shrimp Report, 2014
325 With thanks to Ann Sevier, Chair of Hyde Parish Council & New Forest District Councillor

an established landmark in the 1700's, it can be found marked on older maps as *'Ocknel'* Pond. This is yet another New Forest site which according to legend was visited by Sir Walter Tirel following the murder of William II. The legend goes that Sir Walter Tirel stopped at Ocknell Pond to wash the Kings' blood off his hands and that the pond runs red *'sanguine vermillion'*[326] on the anniversary of the Kings' death. Legend also has it that Ocknell Pond never runs dry[327] (although this isn't actually true!) which accounts for why Sir Walter Tirel was still able to wash his hands in a mist pond in the height of summer.

> *'There will be rain when Sowley's hammer is heard.'*
>
> New Forest Proverb

Other ponds in the New Forest also have legends associated with them. For instance, folklore says that Sowley Pond near Beaulieu is bottomless. Legend tells that the monks from Beaulieu Abbey, who formed the lake in the 1200's, sank a statue made of gold into the pond.[328] Whether or not a golden idol was sunk here is uncertain, but the lake itself is actually relatively shallow and has been drained several times, with no statue found. It is likely that this legend has grown from the ironworks that once stood here, where iron was heated with wood and charcoal from the Forest before being melted and shaped.[329] Gold statues are also mentioned in other places in the New Forest, such as at Sloden inclosure where according to local legend the Romans buried a golden calf.

---

326 The New Forest, Its Traditions, Inhabitants and Customs: De Crespigney & H Hutchinson
327 The Ancient Earthworks of the New Forest: Heywood Sumner
328 The Folklore of Hampshire & the Isle of Wight: Wendy Boase
329 John Richard de Capel Wise: The New Forest, Its History & Its Scenery

GREEN WOOD FIRES:
THE NEVI-WESH ROMANIES

A gypsy told me of a place
Where glow-worms shine as darkness falls
On banks of drove as first owl calls
And moths take flight on wings of lace.

'Contentment' The Romany Way: Irene Sloper

HISTORY OF THE NEVI-WESH ROMANY

The word 'gypsy' comes from the Middle English *gypcian* referring to an inhabitant of Egypt; at one time believed to be the homeland of the Romany Gypsies. However modern research has now proven that the ancestors of the Gypsy originate not in Egypt but northern India, with their earliest written reference in nearby Persia circa 900AD.[330] The Romanies gradually made their way across the globe and into Europe both as slaves and by natural migration, first recorded in the New Forest area amongst the 'cargo' of a ship's transportation documents from 1556.[331] Seeing that the importation of Gypsies was made an offence by an Act of Parliament in 1530, this journey was probably a deportation, but despite these measures Romanies were still making safe passage into Britain. Although first officially recorded in Scotland, the author Len Smith writes it may be likely that the south coast was the 'first landing site' for many Gypsies travelling across from the continent.[332] Indeed, the New Forest was notorious for its surreptitious landing sites and safe passages for smugglers trafficking goods; the same routes could have served the Romany landings well. We later find brief references to Gypsies in the New Forest throughout the 1600's and by the 1800's their numbers are recorded as being in the several

---

330 Romany Nevi-Wesh: Ian Smith
331 Romany Nevi-Wesh: Ian Smith
332 Romany Nevi-Wesh: Ian Smith

hundreds. Len Smith's book, *Romany Nevi-Wesh*, is a must-read for more detail on their history.

The Romanies called the New Forest *Nevi-Wesh* (Romani for 'New Forest'). Although renowned for their nomadic nature, the Gypsies of the New Forest found themselves much at home here. The term 'tent dwelling tribes' was used to describe those Romanies who chose to stay within one district such as the New Forest, moving around within its boundaries between favoured camping grounds. This regular route would usually take approximately 6 weeks and their return was often anticipated by the settled locals, who made use of their skills and bought their wares. Despite misconception, the New Forest Romanies, who sometimes referred to themselves as *Costengris*[333] lived amicably in general alongside their settled neighbours (*Gorjis/Gorgio*, Gypsy term for non-Gypsies) in the New Forest. The treatment of your neighbour was important to a Romany; respect should be given and you will be rewarded.[334] Indeed, RWS Griffith notes in his Hampshire Field Club report *Gipsies of the New Forest* (1893) that they were considered as *'decent, respectable people*[335] and at the very least tolerated, right up until the early 20th century. They had somewhat of a rapport with New Forest locals, themselves living fairly isolated lives in a region that operated not dissimilarly to the Forest Law centuries prior; they too 'a race apart' as the author Brian Vesey-Fitzgerald described (albeit, politically and factually incorrect!). Certainly, the isolation of the woods and moors gave the New Forest Romanies freedom, resources, privacy and some space between themselves and settled communities, who appreciated their skills and wares. Crucially, they were usually tucked away from the authorities who might otherwise move them on. The New Forest has always been a place where social norms and boundaries were quietly rebelled against such as poaching, encroachment (theft of Crown land) and squatting traditions, which were carried out by both settled Foresters and

---

333 New Forest Guidebook, 1934
334 The Romany Way: Irene Soper
335 The Gipsies of the New Forest – Field Meeting 1893: RWS Griffith

Gypsies alike. There are certainly historical references in Court records of New Forest Romanies periodically being implicated in crimes of theft of timber and deer poaching (considered as significant offences in New Forest law) but these misdeeds were in no way exclusive to them. RWS Griffith writes,

> *'they (Gypsies) are certainly not addicted to poaching so much as many of the villagers; and as a consequence, the Forest Keepers rarely have cause to interfere with them.* [336]

Familiar surnames are often found in Romany families right across the UK. Len Smith writes that these names were normally adopted from local families of old stock and usually those of power and wealth; in this way it was sometimes possible to obtain a certain amount of support from that family, or at least hold a name of respectability. [337] More specifically, on the New Forest these surnames included the Eyres, Coopers, Lights, Lovells, Wells and Does; the name Stanley was also common and recognised as a 'royal line' of New Forest Gypsy blood, together with the Lakeys and Lees. [338] As recently as the early 1900's, the New Forest Romanies were also known to have continued to speak in their own native tongue which consisted of thousands of words and phrases occasionally also heard in local Forest dialect. But only relatively recently has the language been written down, when in 1925 a glossary of Romani words collected in the New Forest was published in the *Journal of the Gypsy Lore Society*. This proved to be a difficult task however, since Romani language had until that point only ever been verbal. As such, it is believed that much was over-simplified, or muddled (Romany words muddled with English words, the so-called *'poggadi jib'*)[339] rather than a genuine reflection of a pure dialect. New Forest Romanies were also known for their silent language of *Patrin* (meaning 'scattered leaves') a tradition of roadside codes to point the direction of travel for stragglers or Gypsies arriving later. Examples include small piles of grass, heather or gorse lying nearby one another, or

---

336 The Gipsies of the New Forest – Field Meeting 1893: RWS Griffith
337 Romany Nevi-Wesh: Ian Smith
338 The New Forest: Horace Hutchinson
339 Romany Nevi-Wesh: Ian Smith

crosses drawn in the dirt with the long arm pointing the direction to go.[340] Sticks were also used to point the way to travel. Bent sticks sometimes indicated travellers on foot, whilst branched twigs with a sprig of gorse indicated a family with children. [341]

ROMANY CAMPS

> *The scents of burning leaves and wood-fires hang in the dreaming air like incense, and everywhere there is a delightful haziness from their smoke. The stillness is indescribable, as if nature, now resting, looks on at the richness of her handiwork, well satisfied...Later on, when misty dusk has deepened into darkness, a round yellow moon will rise high above the New Forest and flood the witching scene with the magic of its light.*

'An Autumn Fairytale'
The Enchanted Forest: Gladys M Forbes

At one time, Romany camps were a common sight in the New Forest and as recently as the early 1900's the New Forest Gypsies could be found camping on the Forest in traditional Romany dwellings known as *benders*. [342] Benders were made with green saplings or hazel sticks, bent into hoops to create a semi-circular frame which was then covered with leaves, waxed cloth, oilskins, old carpet or tin. They would often have a small stove inside, with a stack-pipe going out through the top of the tent.[343] The fuel used in the New Forest stoves was normally heather, turf and greenwood and for outdoor cooking, the pot or kettle was stood on a trivet made of horseshoes that stood over an open fire. On some occasions, wealthier families lived in a *vardo* (horse drawn wagons) which also housed a stove, but this was rare in the Forest. When the vardo was used here, it was generally the 'square-bow' style wagon.[344]

Although Romanies could be found anywhere on the Forest, they did have a number of favourite camping sites known to the

---

340 The Romany Way: Irene Soper
341 The Folklore of Hampshire and the Isle of Wight: Wendy Boase
342 The Folklore of Hampshire and the Isle of Wight: Wendy Boase
343 The Romany Way: Irene Soper
344 Romany Nevi-Wesh: Ian Smith

locals at the end of the 19th century. These included Godshill Wood, Crock Hill, Copythorne, Ipley, Ladycross, Norley Wood, Poulner Pits, Picket Post, Burley, Thorney Hill, Shirley Holmes, Pennington, Setley[345] and Chilly Hill.[346] Sites were chosen strategically for materials and supplies, but there was sometimes a little more to it than that. Doreen Valiente writes[347] that certain sites were important in a spiritual way, the 'feel' of the land – a sense that particular places in the Forest were significant, or fortuitous places to live.

> *The Forest Romanies loved the land on Chilly Hill with its coppice firs and its old thorn trees, a place of owls and curlews and wild pony land. The Gypsies in former days had gone there for wild garlic, also camped around that hill, for as old Benny Wells said, 'there can be no 'bitta rickeno poov' (piece of beautiful earth) in the Forest, finer than Chilly Hill. From there a Gypsy can see the sun rise and the sun set, what more can a Gypsy want!*[348]

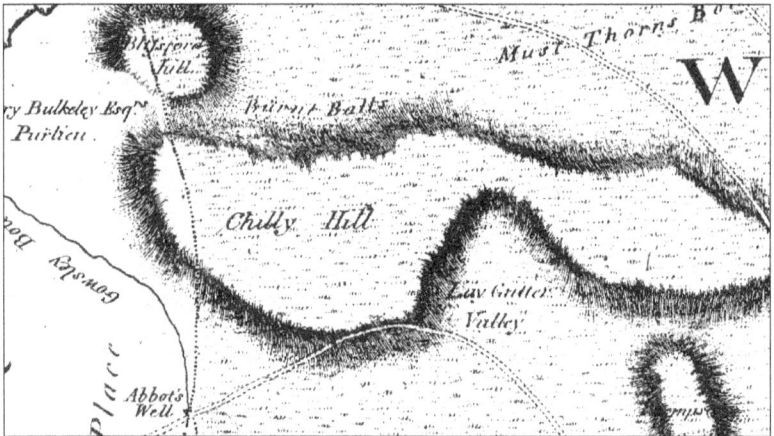

CHILLY HILL, 1789 DRIVERS MAP

---

345 The Gipsies of the New Forest – Field Meeting 1893: RWS Griffith
346 Wanderers in the New Forest: Juliette de Bairacli Levy
347 Witchcraft for Tomorrow: Doreen Valiente
348 Wanderers in the New Forest: Juliette de Bairacli Levy

Romany camps could usually be found amongst the holly bushes or thick undergrowth, pitched by streams or springs. Before the 1900's, the camps were allowed to remain on one site for up to 48 hours, before they were required to move to another spot on the Forest - which they did by hand, on the back of donkeys or by pony and cart. It was common however, for camps to remain pitched in one place for much longer than this if not spotted and ordered to move on.

> *They cook on Sundays their puddings and vegetables with a little pig meat if in luck, or with a tasty roasted hedgehog, or now and then, rabbit.*[349]

The New Forest Romanies were experts at seeking out and using the wild foods of the Forest and meat dishes often included squirrel or *rookomenengro,* which was actually a New Forest delicacy in general. The hunting of squirrel (*squoyling* or *squailing*) was an ancient tradition in the New Forest for the whole community, Gypsy and settled people alike, using a heavy wooden stick with a lead-weighted end (locally known as the *'squadgie', 'snod', 'squoyle'* or *'scogger'*) that was thrown at branches (called *'womping'* the trees) to knock the squirrel to the floor where they would then be caught by net or dog. Squirrel hunting was carried all year round, but was a particular tradition on Boxing Day at which the hunters were summoned to hunt by a horn and concluded at one of the pubs in Brockenhurst, where the squirrels would be made into pies.[350] By the late 1800's attempts had already been made to stop the hunting which was considered both barbaric and detrimental to the population of our native red squirrel and by the early 1900's no more squirrel hunting was allowed in the New Forest while the population of red squirrel remained low. Unfortunately, other than a small population on the nearby Brownsea Island the red squirrel has been almost completely lost to the area due to its already low numbers being pushed out of its habitat by the grey squirrel, which was introduced to the British Isles in the 1890's. However, the term to *'squoyle'* would endure in the New Forest

---

349 The Gipsies of the New Forest – Field Meeting 1893: RWS Griffith
350 Estates Gazette, 1907

becoming an expression of slander (i.e., meaning to cast something negative at another such as an evil glance or a harsh comment). The New Forest Romanies also enjoyed hedgehog *'hotchi-witchi'* (roasted in a ball of clay or over the fire) snails *'bowie'* (toasted on hot ashes with salt or blended and made into soup, *'bowie zoomi'*) and rabbit, with the occasional poached deer or pheasant. The children were known to be expert trout-ticklers.[351] Accompanying these New Forest Romanies enjoyed acorns and beech mast, seasonal fruits and eggs.[352] Other favourites included bracken fronds tied together into bundles and cooked in boiling water then served with butter; and boiled young nettles (so-called 'Gypsy Spinach') blended with wild onions and flaked cereals.[353]

Despite their nomadic heritage, the Romany's love for Nevi-Wesh was such that they put their roots down very firmly where they could. One such place was Nomansland in the north-western part of the Forest, a village that was founded by a Romany named Willet[354]. At the time, the land was not under any ownership and was outside the existing parishes; much like the New Forest tradition of building a 'one-night house' Willet built the first fixed dwelling here in the 18th century and obtained ownership by doing so. Willet was soon joined by other Gypsy families, and the village was created.

> *Aromatic sweet-scented smoke hangs in the windless air...and mingles itself with the autumn mist. Down in a sleepy sheltered hollow is a picturesque encampment of gay-coloured gyspy vans, yellow, green, gold and crimson, decorated with brooms and rush baskets...looking like distorted giant toadstools against the glory of the woods...fragrant with green-wood smoke.'*

'Green-Wood Fires'
from The Enchanted Forest: Gladys M Forbes

---

351 The Romany Way: Irene Soper
352 Horace Hutchinson: The New Forest
353 Irene Soper: New Forest Cookery – Traditional Recipes from a New Forest Cabin
354 Romany Nevi-Wesh: Ian Smith

MAKING A LIVING

The resourceful New Forest Romany could turn their hand to any opportunity. Skills and occupations were often passed down through the family, and the New Forest Romanies had a particular affinity with horse breeding and breaking, charcoal burning, peg and broom making, ferreting rabbits, basket weaving, bee-skep weaving (known as the 'New Forest Pot'[355] and net making. They also took advantage of seasonal materials such as making holly wreaths (cutting was allowed in the New Forest after the 26th November) picking wild watercress, collecting moss for florists, wine making and daffodil picking. In the autumn they could be found collecting wild blackberries and other seasonal fruits for the market or local jam makers.[356] They were also known for making the ash caskets used to make the famous New Forest Mead. Artificial flowers of paper or wood were also well-received; designed in the colours of the New Forest, they were dipped in wax and tied together with sprigs of bog myrtle, broom and cotton grass. Their wares were taken to local markets and fairs or sold to florists and shops. Door to door selling (known as hawking) was also common in the New Forest, and most of the settled locals were usually willing to buy from the Romanies in hope of favour in return (although, others were not so keen and old-fashioned signs saying *'no hawking'* can still be seen on several cottage gates in the New Forest!)

As well as selling their wares, Romany women offered fortune telling (*dukker* or *dukkeripens*).[357] Fortune telling was offered door to door, but most interesting perhaps for the New Forest, at the old Forest gates. Before the introduction of cattle grids in the 1960's, ponies and cattle were kept from straying out of the boundaries by a number of gates and money could be made by standing these gates and offering to open them for traffic, which was a favourite for Gypsy children. One Romany woman named Hannah Lakey was well known for her fortune telling which she

---

355 Hogs at the Honeypot: Frank Vernon
356 The Romany Way: Irene Soper
357 Wanderers in the New Forest: Juliette de Bairacli Levy

offered at the gates to Ornamental Drive, near Rhinefield. Hannah Lakey was known in her time as the 'Queen' of New Forest Gypsies i.e., the matriarch of her encampment and community. When she died in 1903 she was noted as such on the church burial register.[358] Many fortune-telling Romanies were also considered as having the power to curse and cure, the *chovihanic* (witch).[359]

The New Forest Romanies were also known for their snake catching skills (*sapengro*). Harry 'Brusher' Mills, the famous New Forest snake catcher, was often mistaken for a Gypsy, but although he lived in a similar way, he was not in fact a Romany himself.

TRADITIONS & SUPERSTITIONS

Their only God is the God of Nature, whom they thoroughly appreciate. Few people love the Forest more devotedly.

Gipsies of the New Forest: Henry Gibbins

In the UK, Romany travellers generally identify with Christianity and the vast majority consider themselves as Catholic. However, the way each family or community interpret their faith can be vastly different, as well as being hugely influenced by their own Romany folklore. The spirituality of the New Forest Gypsy was formed around a rich cultural history, driven by oral traditions and hereditary superstitions, amulets and magic, especially those surrounding the processes of life and death. As Henry Gibbins writes in his *Gypsies of the New Forest & Other Tales*, despite the New Forest Romanies engaging in the local religious status quo (such as baptising their children and getting married in Church) their dedication to the faith itself was often lip-service at best. Their involvement in the church was, in most cases, encouraged by Missionaries who motivated them with 'perks' they would receive in exchange, such as clothing or financial aid. New Forest Romany wedding ceremonies were

---

358 Romany Nevi-Wesh: Ian Smith
359 Gypsy Sorcery & Fortune Telling: Charles Godfrey Leyland

more likely to involve joining hands, jumping the broomstick[360] or a bed of flowering gorse,[361] or leaping over the fire together.[362] And the blessing of children was often carried out in springs, wells and New Forest mist ponds.

Purity of Blood & Body

Perhaps one of the most important things held close to the Romany's heart is that of their heritage; the honour of pure Romany blood or *kaulo-ratti*, 'black blood'.[363] As such, to assume the title of 'Black' was a Gypsy compliment and in the New Forest, Eliza Cooper held this title as 'Black Liz'. Her uncle, Nehemiah Cooper, was recognised as the King of Hampshire Gypsies.[364] As a general rule, marriage outside of gypsy blood was frowned upon, as recently as the 1940's for this very reason[365] - however Len Smith writes that marriage between Romanies and Gorji did sometimes occur, if the Gorji in question was considered to have a skill or trade that would benefit the Romani community.[366]

The importance of purity to the New Forest Romany extended beyond pure blood to physical cleanliness. For instance *'chikli'* or dirt from the ground (such as soil or other products from nature) was seen as pure, or clean – while *'mochardi'* bodily dirt (such as sweat and menstrual blood) was seen as unclean.[367] This belief is certainly not confined to Gypsy culture, but we see several superstitions surrounding this traditionally essential to the Romany and in the New Forest many seemed to have endured. For instance, women who were menstruating or pregnant were not allowed to cook for others, use the same kitchenware or use the same water sources as the rest of the community. Neither were they allowed to cross these water sources (even by bridge).

---

360 The Folklore of Hampshire and the Isle of Wight: Wendy Boase
361 www.newforestromanygypsytraveller.co.uk
362 The Romany Way: Irene Soper
363 Romany Nevi-Wesh: Ian Smith
364 Wanderers in the New Forest: Juliette de Bairacli Levy
365 Horace Hutchinson: The New Forest
366 Romany Nevi-Wesh: Ian Smith
367 Romany Nevi-Wesh: Ian Smith

There is one account of a pregnant woman in the New Forest having to walk three miles round, just to avoid crossing a stream! [368] However, given that menstruating and pregnant women are considered to be magically potent in many cultures, this superstition may originate from or be conflated with the equally ancient belief that witches cannot cross water.[369]

There were also a number of other superstitions surrounding pregnancy and childbirth, such as a pregnant woman shouldn't wear brand new shoes else it will be the death of the baby; and it was bad luck for a mother to give birth without her ears pierced.[370] Isolation was often also important during childbirth itself. Traditionally, the pregnant woman would be isolated in a separate tent on the outskirts of the camp. Once the baby had been born, all the things that the mother had used during this time were destroyed by fire, often including the tent she gave birth in.[371] And in the north of the New Forest near Fordingbridge, there are accounts of it being customary for women to give birth out in the wilds, under a particular holly tree on Godshill Ridge (now the Roger Penny Way route).

I keep each one within my heart,
As time goes by and we're apart.
I long to be united still
With the 'Gypsies of Godshill'.

Though I cannot turn back the hands of time
I can travel in my mind,
To a place where time stands still,
And join the Gypsies on Godshill.

My Heritage, Godshill Gypsies: Karen Griswold

This isolation of child-birthing women is something that appears to have died out during the late 20th century in the New Forest; Irene Soper, who wrote about the New Forest gypsies in 1994, describes how babies were born in a van or tent.[372] Despite

---

368 Paultons Romany Life & Customs
369 John Richard de Capel Wise: The New Forest, Its History & Its Scenery
370 www.newforestromanygypsytraveller.co.uk
371 The Folklore of Hampshire and the Isle of Wight: Wendy Boase
372 My New Forest Home: Irene Soper

the superstitious stigma surrounding women, the New Forest Romany communities were largely matriarchally led. For instance, it was considered acceptable for a woman to keep her maiden name when she married and therefore many Romany surnames were matriarchally inherited. Women were also often in charge of the camp movement with travel dictated by where women were hawking their goods or collecting supplies,[373] wild food and herbal cures.

Just as belongings were destroyed at the beginning of a life, so too were they destroyed at the end of a life. Usually, a Gypsy was cremated together with their worldly possessions, both for the purpose of sending them to the afterlife but also off the back of the belief that the ghost of the deceased would not leave the camp while their possessions remained. Horse brasses, considered as personal charms, were also destroyed during this process and food was also laid out for the dead to take into the afterlife.[374] Horses owned by the deceased were usually sold out of the family.[375]

The fear of *mulos* (ghost, or *bavol-angro* 'wind fellow') was strong amongst the Romany community and resulted in death-vigils over the dead body before burial or cremation to guard against the ghost leaving the body, with candles laid near the bed of the dying to guide them into the next world.[376] In the New Forest, Frank Cuttriss[377] observed a number of 'watchers' being involved in this during one vigil and being switched regularly so that they didn't lose focus; so strong was their concern of being haunted, '*mulleno*'. Bread could be carried in the pocket to protect against ghosts and malign spirits[378] and it was customary for a rose or thorn bush to be planted over a Gypsy grave to prevent the dead from rising.[379] Nettles were also seen as protecting against

---

373 Romany Nevi-Wesh: Ian Smith
374 The Folklore of Hampshire and the Isle of Wight: Wendy Boase
375 The Pattern Under The Plough: George Ewart Evans
376 www.newforestromanygypsytraveller.co.uk
377 Romany Life: Frank Cuttriss
378 The Romany Way: Irene Soper
379 The Folklore of Hampshire and the Isle of Wight: Wendy Boase

the walking dead and Romany lore describes that nettles are found growing near the entrances to the underworld[380] presumably to stop souls from passing into the world of the living. Another interesting Gypsy custom surrounding death can be found in the New Forest village of Woodgreen. It was customary for a Romany who died suddenly or far from home to be buried where the event occurred; called a *'hedge burial'*.[381] Here at Woodgreen there are two crosses on the ground where as local lore would have it, two Gypsies killed each other in a fight and were buried on the spot.[382]

The New Forest Romanies held a wealth of oral superstitions which had been passed down the generations; animals were of particular interest and perhaps most fitting for the New Forest was the horse. To the Romanies, horses were sacred and in the New Forest a ring made from plaited horsehair was worn as a lucky charm. It was particularly lucky if made from the hair of a piebald or skewbald horse and especially a stallion.[383] It was also considered good luck if you saw a horse with its head over a gate![384] Another animal that featured heavily in Romany lore was the frog or toad, especially in Gypsy magic and fortune telling. Charles Leyland writes[385] that the Romany dialect for 'toad' finds its roots in the same word for the word *devil* and it appears that much of Gypsy toad magic or superstition is that of taming or controlling the behaviour of the toad, presumably thereby controlling the power of the devil. A tame toad was said to assist in fortune-telling and in the New Forest a frog hopping onto the wagon steps was considered a good omen.[386] Snails were also used in Romany magic and considered to represent darkness, their 'horns' akin to the horns of the devil. The term devil otherwise referred to the old horned gods, often those diminished to lesser spirits and demi-gods such as *Puck/Pooka*. Charles Leyland writes

---

380 Gypsy Sorcery & Fortune Telling: Charles Godfrey Leyland
381 www.newforestromanygypsytraveller.co.uk
382 Wanderers in the New Forest: Juliette de Bairacli Levy
383 The Folklore of Hampshire and the Isle of Wight: Wendy Boase
384 Paultons Romany Life & Customs
385 Gypsy Sorcery & Fortune Telling: Charles Godfrey Leyland
386 Paultons Romany Life & Customs

that in some Gypsy communities the snail was described as something that roughly equates to *'Pucks Horse'* or similar. Given the fondness for Puck and the Pixy Colt in the New Forest, its likely the New Forest Romany believed this too. The snail was used in charms for exorcism and protection against malign magic[387] it seems to me in a similar way to the toad; by controlling the snail one controlled the power of the devil. Although there are accounts of snails being killed as part of Gypsy magic[388] in general it was considered bad luck to kill a snail in Romany lore.[389] They did however feature in the diet of the New Forest Gypsy, salted snails being a favourite – so whether this particular superstition wasn't followed in the Forest, or whether it was overlooked for the sake of a good dinner, we may never know! Bees coming into the tent or wagon were also lucky, as well as a robin or long-tailed tit tapping on the wagon window (what the birds are probably doing is collecting spiderweb for their nests). The snake and the weasel were also considered good omens; of course, there were a number of bad omens too including an owl hooting after dawn, a cuckoo heard after midsummer and the sound of a falling tree.[390] It was also unlucky to call a rat, 'a rat'. Should you accidently do so, you could avert the bad luck by shouting *'Beng Beng Beng Beng!'*[391] In Romany lore, *Beng* is the devil, who is said to dwell in the woods[392] or in an underworld made of compacted mud.[393] Everyday objects were also the source of some superstition for the New Forest Gypsy. For instance, it is very unlucky to walk between a Gypsy and their *yog* (fire).[394] Nor should snowdrops be brought inside the tent or van[395] and despite the title of 'Black' being a Romany compliment the colour itself was often considered unlucky and black clothes were not

387 Gypsy Sorcery & Fortune Telling: Charles Godfrey Leyland
388 Gypsy Sorcery & Fortune Telling: Charles Godfrey Leyland
389 Paultons Romany Life & Customs
390 Paultons Romany Life & Customs
391 www.newforestromanygypsytraveller.co.uk
392 The Gypsies: Jean Paul Clebert
393 Dictionary of Gypsy Life & Lore: Harry Wedeck
394 The Romany Way: Irene Soper
395 The Romany Way: Irene Soper

generally worn, instead being borrowed when needed.[396] Nor should blankets be washed during the month of May, for it will wash your family away; children's hair should not be cut until their second birthday and fingernails must not be cut on Sunday.[397]

Living teeth and jowl on the land also gave the Gypsies an indelible connection and understanding of the natural world and what it could provide. Irene Soper gives several examples in her book *The Romany Way*, such as an ointment for swelling made of worms and a treatment for deafness made from the fat of a hedgehog.[398] Their understanding of the natural world crossed into the esoteric too with *dukker*, charms, blessings and curses a speciality for some New Forest Romany families known for their *chovihanic* abilities. Many folk cures were known the New Forest Romany, such as banishing warts (by impaling a black slug onto the spines of a blackthorn bush, as the slug shrivels so does the wart)[399] or offering protection by way of a shoestring kept upon the person as an amulet.[400] In other situations, a shoestring could be taken to secure protection (for instance Romanies were often wary of having their photo taken, but if a shoelace was given in exchange for the image, it eliminated any risk).[401] Equally, a sprig of gorse carried on the person would keep away a fever and rosemary hung in the tent or van would ward off evil.[402] Simple blessings and curses were also common. The New Forest author Irene Soper writes how she herself was blessed as a baby by one Granny Sheen who lived in a compound near Irene's home; but also gives details of cases where curses had been placed by Gypsies due to fallouts and misunderstandings. At least two examples given by Irene led to almost immediate illness and death.[403]

---

396 Wanderers in the New Forest: Juliette de Bairacli Levy
397 www.newforestromanygypsytraveller.co.uk
398 The Romany Way: Irene Soper
399 The Romany Way: Irene Soper
400 Dictionary of Gypsy Life & Lore: Harry Wedeck
401 Gypsy Sorcery & Fortune Telling: Charles Godfrey Leyland
402 The Romany Way: Irene Soper
403 The Romany Way: Irene Soper

Their understanding of the natural world on an esoteric level also meant that the New Forest Romanies would also become influential in the modern witchcraft movement, which blossomed in the New Forest area during the early 1900's. They formed friendships with people such as Katherine Oldmeadow, whose book *Folklore of Herbs* (1946) was stacked with material gleaned from the gypsies at Thorney Hill, and her friend Dorothy Clutterbuck who would become significant in the resurgence of witchcraft in the New Forest area. I personally believe these friendships were the result of philanthropic work bringing them in contact with Gypsy women.

> *'Miss Oldmeadow had many friends among the Gypsies, in whom she took a great interest and when she wrote a book about herbs – another subject in which she took great interest – they were able to supply her with some of the material for the book.*[404]

The New Forest Gypsies became friends with a number of local authors throughout the years, themselves somewhat wild women who would preserve the spirit of the Forest and its Romany inhabitants, such as Joan Bairacli-Levy who was host to a number of Gypsies in her New Forest cottage and wrote *Wanderers of the New Forest,* Irene Soper who was aided with her book *The Herbal Handbook* by Eliza Cooper and Sybil Leek, author of *Diary of a Witch* and *A Shop on the High Street,* who often traded with Romanies from her antiques shop in Ringwood.

A CHANGING LANDSCAPE

> *We have given our hearts away, a sordid boon!*
> *This sea that bares her bosom to the moon,*
> *the winds that will be howling at all hours*
> *and are up-gathered now like sleeping flowers,*
> *for this, for everything, we are out of tune;*
> *it moves us not...*

The World Is Too Much With Us:,
William Wordsworth

---

404 Obituary, Christchurch Times 12th July 1963

In the late 1800's and early 1900's, charitable philanthropists and clergymen had been working to reduce the number of tent-dwelling families in the New Forest, offering to arrange for them employment, fixed housing and education. The offer was accepted by a number of Romany families however many would refuse (or otherwise, accept a house only to flee back into the Forest shortly after). One case describes a ninety-year-old woman named Mrs Sherred who was gifted a cottage in Bull Hill near Boldre. She stole back into the Forest soon after and was later tracked down camping amongst the holly bushes of Shirley Holmes. When asked why, she declared, *I couldn't abide that 'ere roof over my 'ed. I couldn't bide it no hows. If I'd stopt there another day I should have died.* [405]

But things were changing for the New Forest in the 1900's. With improvements to roads and other methods of travel visitors to the Forest were increasing and as such the desirability of the area started to rise. Many properties that had otherwise been Forest cottages with commoning rights started to be bought as holiday and retirement homes by people from outside the area. Although the Romanies added to the 'magic' of the New Forest for many visitors, living amongst them was a somewhat different experience for those people who had moved from the cities and as such, the Romanies of the New Forest began to be regarded as somewhat of an 'unsightly problem'. Perhaps due to this change in dynamics and the increasing number of complaints by residents against Romanies, an Act was passed in 1926 which stated that to camp on open Forest was now an offence. In response, the Office of Woods and Forests (now The Forestry Commission) created seven 'compounds 'across the New Forest where Romanies were permitted to camp; these included sites at Blackhamsley, Broomhill, Hardley, Latchmoor, Longdown, Thorney Hill and Shave Wood. Each compound (since compared by several writers as being akin to 'concentration camps') usually held 8-15 families. [406] Here they put up their normal bender tents although

---

405 Gipsies of the New Forest: Henry Gibbins
406 Gipsy Missioning in the New Forest, 1934

they also started to use more fixed materials like wood frameworks and tin roofs. Some compounds were fenced and others were not. Movement between compounds was not exactly restricted but camping outside compounds was not allowed,[407] many families moved into the compounds with little resistance, but there are accounts that a number were forcibly moved or coerced.[408]

Whilst removing the immediate 'problem' of the New Forest Gypsies from general view, these compounds would prove to be at the cost of their health and general wellbeing. Previously nomadic, the Romanies were used to moving from one place to another, always on rested, dry ground with renewed natural supplies. But now they were forced to camp in one place which led to depleted materials and muddy, slum-like conditions. No facilities whatsoever were provided, causing them to travel to neighbouring villages to use their water and other facilities. The ongoing pressure felt by local villagers to share their local resources began to wear thin.[409] The local artist Augustus Edwin John, friend of the Romanies and known to them as 'Sir Gustus'[410] wrote *in the groundworm-infested filth of the New Forest concentration camps, they are condemned to squalor, disease and degradation.*'

At the beginning of WW2 these seven camps were reduced to five, which exacerbated the problem. In 1945, further plans were made for the camp inhabitants to begin living in abandoned WW2 bases, which were numerous on the Forest including at Holmsley and Ibsley however, these proved to be as unsanitary as the compounds and further consultations were held which even suggested the entire removal of the population to at least 5 miles outside of the boundaries of the Forest. In the 1950's a number of prefabricated bungalows were erected to house some of the families, with sites including North Baddesley and Thorney Hill. [411] Understandably this whole resettlement process was a

407 Gipsies of the New Forest: Henry Gibbins
408 Romany Nevi-Wesh: Ian Smith
409 Romany Nevi-Wesh: Ian Smith
410 The Romany Way: Irene Soper
411 The Folklore of Hampshire and the Isle of Wight: Wendy Boase

considerable adjustment for families, who for generations had enjoyed freedom and a minimalistic lifestyle. Especially for the children - one account describes how one family had only been in their new house for an hour or two before the children started ripping the paper off the walls.[412] With the passing of the 1959 Highway Act, it became an offence to camp on the roadside, making travel in and out of the New Forest more difficult and in 1965 a housing plan was created to move all families from their temporary accommodation into council housing or otherwise, wooden cabins and static caravans on the edge of the Forest and common land.

---

412 Gipsies of the New Forest: Henry Gibbins

LOST & ICONIC BEASTS
OF THE FOREST

THE ADDER

Deep in heather, coiled in gorse, sunk among
the winter stones
For adder is as adder hisses ...

The Lost Words, A Spell Book:
Robert Macfarlane & Jackie Morris

The adder is one of three native snakes living in the New Forest along with the smooth snake and the ringed snake, but the adder is the only one with venom. The adder is difficult to spot as its instinct is to flee at the first sign of being disturbed; however, in the right circumstances it is possible. As a child, I remember sneaking into the Forest in the early morning to the sight of dozens of adders, all coiled up on the emmet-mounds warming up in the morning sun. If you are quiet, is also possible to spot them in certain places in the New Forest, camouflaged amongst the heather and bracken. It is not recommended to tread quietly through the scrub during adder season however, as they will bite if surprised.

Snake catching was somewhat of a vocation in the New Forest, for the purpose of culling adders from private land, selling to collectors or zoos as exhibits and to make cures for snake bites and other ailments. In the New Forest, folk remedies for adder bites included 'adder balm' made from the fat of adders as well as an even stranger cure which involved a bag compress containing the heads of an adder, a toad and a newt. The bag of three heads was soaked and then applied to the bite. This cure was used as recently as the 19th century.[413] Snake catching was offered as a service by the New Forest Gypsies, but a more well-known character associated with snake-catching was Harry 'Brusher' Mills (1840-1905), the famous New Forest snake catcher who

---

413 www.newforestnpa.gov.uk

Crespigney & Hutchinson wrote always caught them by hand, behind their head between his thumb and forefinger.[414] He was made famous in the New Forest for capturing adders, although his trade was mainly in the ringed and smooth snake. Throughout his career he claimed to have caught 29,402 snakes and 4,124 adders (33,526 animals in total).[415] He is also rumoured to have made the wooden chair with ornate snake carvings which can be seen in the New Forest Heritage Centre Museum in Lyndhurst. Harry lived in an old charcoal-burner's hut near Brockenhurst, and being somewhat of a recluse, was often mistaken for a Gypsy, although not of Gypsy blood himself. He was evicted from this hut after 20 years, at 63 years old, for 'various reasons', and after a while the cabin was destroyed.[416] A similar character - simply known as Bob - caught snakes, owls and other curiosities in the New Forest for collectors.[417]

The adder even found itself part of a small piece of New Forest folklore; the short tale is about a little girl who shared her breakfast with an adder, but the snake ate more than his share. The legend is the origin of the local expression *'eat your own side, speckleback'* which is used to scold greedy people.[418]

> *There was bred in Hampshire neere Bistherne a devouring Dragon, who doing much mischief upon men and cattell and could not be destroyed but spoiled many in attempting it, making his den neere unto a Beacon. This Sir Moris Barkley armed himself and encountered with it and at length overcam and killed it but died himself soone after.*
>
> – 15th century account from the records of Berkeley Castle

In folklore and mythology, the term 'snake' or 'worm' was often used to describe a dragon or dragon-like creature, and so this chapter could not be complete without mentioning the New Forest's very own Dragon of Bisterne. According to local

---

414 The New Forest, Its Traditions, Inhabitants and Customs: De Crespigney & H Hutchinson
415 Gerald Lascelles Deputy Surveyor (14: Christopher Tower Reference Library)
416 Gerald Lascelles Deputy Surveyor (14: Christopher Tower Reference Library)
417 The New Forest, Its Traditions, Inhabitants and Customs: De Crespigney & H Hutchinson
418 John Richard de Capel Wise: The New Forest, Its History & Its Scenery

legend, the dragon would swoop from its lair on Burley Rocks or Burley Beacon and terrorise the village of Bisterne, demanding pails of milk and the flesh of cattle.[419]

Together with his hunting dogs named Grim and Holdfast, Sir Maurice Berkeley set about to slay the dragon, a battle which began in Dragon Fields at Lower Bisterne Farm. The dragon was eventually slain at Boltons Bench in Lyndhurst, the arch of its back creating the hill at the centre of the green. A broken man following his battle with the dragon, Berkley died at the dragons' side and his yew-wood bow sprouted the Yew trees that grow on top of the hill today.[420] A depiction of Berkeley's two dogs can be seen carved above the doorway of Bisterne Park Manor House.

Although outside the bounds of the New Forest, another Hampshire myth tells of the Cockatrice of Wherwell, a monstrous creature described as having the wings of a bird or bat, the head of a cockerel and the tail of a snake or dragon. The Cockatrice had a taste for human flesh and, according to local lore, was hatched by a toad from a duck egg in the crypt of Wherwell Abbey. It was eventually slain by a local man named Green, who was rewarded with 4 acres of land; and according to folklorist Cecilia Millson, the villagers of Wherwell have never eaten duck eggs since![421]

THE WHITE HART: DEER OF THE NEW FOREST

Vital to the survival of our ancient ancestors, deer were often considered as sacred. They were portrayed in therianthropic cave art (*therianthrope* from the Greek therion 'wild beast' and *anthropos* 'man'), the depiction of the sympathetic magic practiced across Europe in which hunters and magic workers would imitate their prey.[422] An example of this practice is an antlered red deer skull headdress found at Star Carr in Yorkshire, c. 8000 BCE; together with a fur hide; the headdress would also have allowed the hunter

---

419 The Folklore of Hampshire & the Isle of Wight: Wendy Boase
420 New Forest Hauntings: Richard Reeves
421 Tales of Old Hampshire, Cecilia Millson
422 Craft of the Wise: Vikki Bramshaw

to blend in with his quarry.[423] Deer continued to be an important resource throughout history and would remain a symbol of abundance, depicted in jewellery and family crests and symbolic of royal blood, nobility and privilege.

There are five different types of deer living in the New Forest: the Red, the Fallow, the Roe, the Sika and the Muntjac. The Sika and Muntjac were introduced in the 1900's but the Roe are native to the British Isles as is the Fallow, a long-standing resident who was established here during the Roman period. The Red is native to the British Isles but has never populated the Forest in great numbers; Gerald Lascelles, Deputy Surveyor 1800-1914, stated that Red *'should not be reckoned in speaking of Forest deer proper.'*[424] Deer certainly have an important place in the history of the area. Described as one of the architects of the New Forest, the deer were instrumental in an ecological sense, but also as the primary quarry of the King's hunt, preserving the Forest from possible exploitation by other means. An integral part of the landscape and its ecosystem, the deer found an important place in the folklore in the New Forest and several places are also named after them, such as Roe Wood near Linford and Deer Leap near Lyndhurst, where local folklore says a pursued stag covered eighteen yards in a single bound.[425]

Pale deer were considered particularly mysterious, thought to be omens or messengers from the otherworld,[426] and known to be one of the many forms of the New Forest Colt Pixy. A white deer was also a prized hunting quarry for the King, especially the white stag, known as the *White Hart.* Local legend recalls that a White Hart was captured in the New Forest by Henry VII. The stag (according to some accounts, named 'Albert')[427] gave such a good chase that the King spared the animal and collared it with a band of gold, after which it was led to Ringwood. A similar tale from Blackmore Vale in the neighbouring county of Dorset

---

423 The British Museum, London
424 British Deer & their Horns: John G Millais
425 The Folklore of Hampshire and the Isle of Wight: Wendy Boase
426 Woodland Folk Tales of Britain and Ireland: Lisa Schneidau
427 The Book of the Axe: George Pulman

describes how the collar was engraved with *'I am a Royal Hart, let no one harm me.'*[428] The motif of the white stag in a golden collar is not confined to Wessex. Pliny writes that Alexander the Great caught and collared a White Hart, whilst Aristotle describes how the Greek hero Diomedes dedicated a White Hart with a golden collar to the goddess Diana. Another comparable legend exists in Berkshire's Windsor Forest.[429] Incidentally, the 'white hart' was also the name of a royal collar worn by royalty, a pendant engraved with the image of the collared stag either worn like a brooch or hung from a golden collar formed in the shape of broom seedpods.[430]

A ghostly White Hart is said to roam the woods of Bolderwood, whilst in 1962 a local resident named Ruth Tongue wrote that her great-uncle (a New Forest Verderer) spoke of a huge phantom stag that always appeared in the Forest before the death of a sovereign. The stag was also known to have appeared to a handful of Verderers over the years (who, according to her great-uncle, had later all suffered violent deaths).[431] Certainly, the deer of the New Forest have ghostly associations, and may also be linked with phantom hunters. One legend originating in the neighbouring county of Berkshire recalls a Forest Keeper named Herne, who was suspected of poaching in Windsor Forest during the reign of Richard II. Legend has it that with shame and fear he hung himself on an old oak, destined to haunt the tree forevermore.[432] Other tales describe how Herne was almost killed by a stag but saved by a magician named Philip Urswick, who brought him back to life by binding the decapitated head of the stag upon Herne. However, the other Keepers - who had always been envious of Herne's skill - bartered with the magician to curse Herne. He lost his skill for hunting shortly afterwards and, with shame, hung himself on the old oak tree. However, with a curse there is usually a catch, and after Herne's death the curse was

---

428 Knowledge for the People: John Timbs
429 The History of Signboards: J Larwood & J Hotton
430 The Gentleman's Magazine and Historical Chronicle (Vol 171) 1842
431 The Folklore of Hampshire and the Isle of Wight: Wendy Boase
432 A Treatise on the Identity of Herne's Oak: W Perry, 1867

passed onto the very Keepers who had ordered it who were forced by magical means to join Herne for a ghostly wild hunt.[433]

'With great rag'd horns,
He blasts the tree and takes the cattle
And makes milch-kine yield blood and shakes a chain
In a most hideous and dreadful manner.'[434]

Probably inspired by local legend, the first written record of Herne was made by Shakespeare in his *Merry Wives of Windsor,* who described him as a terrifying phantom who haunted the Royal Forest during the winter months. Descriptions of his ghost are usually anthropomorphic, a man wearing antlers and riding a foulsome black horse. He is also sometimes accompanied by two black hounds[435] with red ears[436] - spectral black dogs, which, according to wider folklore, often act as harbingers of bad omens or death. Other records suggest that Herne is a forest demon, who pursues Keepers to sell their souls to him[437] or that his ghost roams the Forest in the shape of *"a great stag",*[438] foretelling serious hardship or death. This perhaps resembles the New Forest stag as described by Ruth Tongue in 1962. Herne's appearance is also associated with minor misfortunes, such as spoiling milk and bewitching animals - the sort of bad luck usually attributed to lesser spirits such as imps or fairies.

Although the legend of Herne was originally confined to Berkshire, his name is intimately familiar to many in the New Forest, where he is generally considered a local spirit or demi-god. Jacob Grimm writes in his *Deutsche Mythologie* (1835) that Herne was likely conflated with the deity Woden, leader of the Wild Hunt of Norse origin and whose cult was firmly established in southern Britain by the Anglo-Saxons. Grimm suggests that, like Woden, Herne came to be considered as the leader of his own ghostly hunt, haunting the skies above the British Isles.

433 The Forest in Folklore and Mythology: Alexander Porteous
434 Shakespeare's Merry Wives of Windsor
435 The Forest in Folklore and Mythology: Alexander Porteous
436 The Witches' God: Janet and Stewart Farrar
437 The Forest in Folklore and Mythology: Alexander Porteous
438 Shakespeare's Merry Wives of Windsor (early pirated edition)

Additionally, Sorita d'Este and David Rankine suggest in their book *Isles of the Many Gods* that the name Herne may have been used as a shortening of *Herian*, a title of Woden.[439]

By the 1600's the enthusiasm to restrict Royal Forests exclusively for hunting had begun to waver, and the Crown's interest in the Forest became redirected towards the production of timber. With the decline in hunting, the deer began to suffer from overpopulation which reduced the grazing available to other animals. In 1851 the Deer Removal Act was established as a measure to control the overpopulation by culling the deer of the Forest; Lascelles describes how *'bobbery packs of hounds and guns of every description were called into service.'*[440] The Forest Laws of Winter Heyning and Fence Month, periods when stock usually in the Forest should be removed for the benefit of the deer, were also abandoned.[441] The deer have endured, however; still existing in great numbers in the New Forest although often remaining unseen - just a fleeting glimpse as they dash into the undergrowth of a dozen wagging white tails in the far distance.

THE MARTEN

In old Forest Law the pine marten, 'marten cat' or 'matron' was at times counted as one of the *Beasts of Venery* - an animal hunted in the New Forest along with others such as deer, boar and hare.[442] The Marten is a small mammal with a chocolate-brown pelt and yellow throat, bushy tail and almost bear-like facial features and paws. The animal is most active during dusk and night-time and therefore, like so many other secretive nocturnal creatures, came to be viewed with some superstition. According to some legends, the marten's bushy tail hides a deadly spine or claw, although in other cases it was considered a lucky charm, perhaps due to its skill and intelligence. It was also considered to be a trickster; in some parts of the world the marten was held responsible for weaving plaits in the manes of horses

439 Isles of the Many Gods: Sorita d'Este & David Rankine
440 35 Years in the New Forest: Gerald Lascelles
441 The New Forest: Rose C De Crespigny & Horace Hutchinson
442 The New Forest: Horace Hutchinson

overnight,[443] with a similar superstition surviving here in the Forest of rough wind-plaits or 'elf locks' believed to be woven by unseen spirits.

This is that very Mab
That plaits the manes of horses in the night
And bakes the elf-plaits in foul sluttish hairs
Which, once untangled, much misfortune bodes.
Shakespeare's Romeo & Juliet

The marten was once widespread across Britain, but by 1900 the animal was all but extinct due to hunting and loss of habitat. However, more recently, the marten has enjoyed a comeback in some secluded areas of the UK including the New Forest, where it favours leafy deciduous woodland and the coniferous inclosures.

J MEYDENBACH, 1491

THE NIGHT HAWK (NIGHTJAR)

The night hawk is singing his frog-like tune,
Twirling his watchman's rattle about.
William Wordsworth – The Waggoner

The nightjar, a summer visitor to the New Forest, is surrounded by mystery and superstition. The bird arrives from warmer climates at the beginning of May, and although they can

---

443 Pine Martens: Johnny Birks

be found elsewhere in Britain, they particularly favour the New Forest, nesting here in greater numbers. It is an unusual-looking creature, hawk-like in appearance, earning it local New Forest names of *Night Hawk, Ground Hawk*,[444] *Dew-Hawk* or *Dor Hawk*. Taking to the wing at the liminal times of dawn and dusk, it twists and turns silently in the air, resembling a bird of prey in its flight to catch insects on the wing, in a technique described as 'hawking'. They will also hover like a hawk over predators such as foxes and will mob them if necessary.[445] The nightjar has a huge and gaping whale-like mouth, ideal for catching insects on the wing, which virtually stretches from ear to ear and adds to the bizarre, otherworldly appearance of this bird. It also benefits from bark-like plumage which offers a camouflage so effective it's virtually impossible to spot.

The nightjar is known for its strange nocturnal song - a trilling, whirling call often mistaken for frogs or crickets. The correct term is 'churring'[446] or 'to chur', which earns it two other folk names, the *Night Churr* or the *Churn Owl*. When in flight, they also make a soft 'coo-ic' and a whip-crack sound with their wings[447] which has earned it its other folk name, *Whip-Poor-Will*. Our ancestors found these bizarre sounds (and the creature that made them) rather ominous. Even Wordsworth described the unseen nightjar's song as *'the spirit of a toil-worn slave, lashed out of life, not quiet in the grave'*.[448] As such, the nightjar quickly became associated with death, liminality and the chthonic, and a feared and unseen beast of the moors, which earned it another folk name, the *Lich Fowle* or corpse bird. Other folk names for the nightjar are *Night Crow, Fern Owl,* and *Jossy Grigory*. But perhaps the strangest legend of the nightjar surrounds another of its folk names, the *Goat Sucker* or *Goat Chaffer,* which originates from the belief that the Nightjar steals milk from the udders of goats, cattle and sheep. As a result, they were often blamed for low milk yields. It is likely this

---

444 John Richard de Capel Wise: The New Forest, Its History & Its Scenery
445 Nightjars: Cleere & Nurney
446 Readers Digest Book of British Birds
447 Readers Digest Book of British Birds
448 A Morning Exercise, 1828: William Wordsworth

superstition arose from the habit of the Nightjar of visiting pastures and animal sheds at dusk to prey on midges and other insects. It is also possible that the shape of their mouth seemed perfect for drinking from the udder.[449] This belief was so ingrained that it was immortalised in the Nightjar's Latin name, *caprimulgus europaeus*, from '*caper*' goat, and '*mulego*' milk.

Another bird that finds itself part of New Forest folklore is the Cuckoo, the herald of spring to the Forest which reaches our shores around mid-April. The arrival of spring was marked by the Beaulieu Fair on the 15th of April (known as *Cuckoo Day*)[450] and the Cuckoo Fair at Downton during the May Day Bank Holiday.

'The cuckoo goes to Beaulieu Fair to buy him a petticoat.'[451]

– New Forest proverb

'The cuckoo comes in April and stays the month of May, sings a song at midsummer, and then goes away.'[452]

– Proverb from the nearby county of Wiltshire

BEES & BEEKEEPING

A swarm of bees in May is worth a load of hay.

New Forest proverb

The New Forest was famous for its honey, being the perfect environment for bees, with its vast swathes of heather, gorse flowers and fruit blossoms. As a result, honey production has a particularly long season here due to the late-blooming heather flowers. Early in the season, the honey tends to be from oak blossom, which doesn't make a particularly nice honey, but in the later months the bees are able to take advantage of a wide range of flowers and clover, with the most valued honey coming from the late summer and autumn heather bloom.[453] As such, beekeeping is an ancient tradition in the New Forest. Shards of Iron Age pottery beehives have been found at Gorley Hill, and

449 The Helm Dictionary of Scientific Bird Names
450 John Richard de Capel Wise: The New Forest, Its History & Its Scenery
451 Dictionary of Proverbs: George L Apperson
452 Dictionary of Proverbs: George L Apperson
453 The New Forest, Its Traditions, Inhabitants and Customs: De Crespigney & H Hutchinson

until the early part of the 1900's bee swarms were still being kept in the hollow trunks of ancient trees or wooden posts in the New Forest.[454] Bees were also housed in hives in the open Forest in 'bee gardens', square enclosures created with banked earth (often recalled in place names on the OS map, such as *'Bee Garn'*) to keep the stock away from the hives. Beekeepers are still allowed to use the open Forest today, with permission.

Very little honey was imported into the area; as an example, in the 13th century at least 300 hives were kept in the area of the small village of Beaulieu alone. Most households had a hive for their own personal use, and De Crespigny and Hutchinson wrote in the 1800's *'almost every Forester is a beekeeper.*[455] The most popular hive was the 'skep', a conical hive made from woven straw with a thatch or *'hackle'*, yet the Forest had its own design, the *New Forest Pot*, which was made by the local Gypsies out of sedge and bound with brambles.[456] Unfortunately, neither of these hives were robust, lasting 2-3 years at best, and the only way to remove the honey without destroying the skep was to destroy the colony, often by *'stipple'* (sulphur) or as recorded at Abbots Well, by submerging the skep into water.[457] Today, hives are made with removable frames and no bees are harmed when the honey is removed: the frames are simply taken out and the bees gently 'smoked' off. The frames are then spun in a separator to remove the honey from the *workings* (the New Forest term for honeycomb). The frames with eggs and grubs remain in the lower portion of the hive, and the bees are always left with enough honey to feed them.

The New Forest has its own native honeybee called the New Forest Black, a strain of the British Black Bee *apis mellifera mellifera*. The British Black was almost extinct by the early 1900's, but since has been enjoying a gradual revival with beekeepers as its honey is particularly delicious! In the past, Keepers were also able to

---

454 Hogs at the Honeypot: Frank Vernon
455 The New Forest, Its Traditions, Inhabitants and Customs: De Crespigney & H Hutchinson
456 Hogs at the Honeypot: Frank Vernon
457 Wanderers in the New Forest: Juliette de Bairacli Levy

collect honey from wild bee colonies.[458] The Forest also has its fair share of wild ground-nesting bees, some are solitary whilst others live in colonies. We had a colony living in the earth bank that surrounds our parking space last year, and we managed to live with them very peacefully - even getting up close to watch them fly in and out of their nest.

There is a wealth of folklore surrounding the bee, and the New Forest has its fair share. For instance, they were seen as an indicator of the coming harvest, such as the old saying *'a swarm of bees in May is worth a load of hay'* – i.e., the more bees seen during late spring and early summer, the better hay harvest later in the year. Customs also surrounded the husbandry of bees in the New Forest. Before housing a new colony, the inside of the hive was often rubbed down with crushed balm, honeywort or marjoram. These herbs are particularly attractive to bees and were believed to help encourage the new colony adopt the hive as their own rather than swarm (ie, to leave the hive). Bees in the process of swarming were described as being under an enchantment, and the old New Forest saying *'like a swarm of bees all in a charm'* may have come about from this. Below is an extract from an Anglo-Saxon spell, the 'Wið Ymbe Charm' for *'bringing down'* or *'tanging'* swarms (i.e., encouraging them to settle down rather than fly further away), found in the margins of an 11th-century manuscript:

> *'Against a swarm of bees, take earth, throw with your right hand under thy right foot, and say, "I catch under foot, I found it. Lo, earth avails against all creatures whatever ..." then throw over them sand, and say,*

> *"Settle down, wise-women, sink to the earth Never ye to wild wood fly. Be as mindful of my welfare As is each man of meat and home."*

In the New Forest, beekeepers were known to communicate with their bees or *'brownies'* by humming a particular sound or tune when they wanted to work with them, which the bees came to

---

458 John Richard de Capel Wise: The New Forest, Its History & Its Scenery

know,[459] and keepers would say they came to know the mood of their bees by the sound of their buzzing.[460] It was also customary in Hampshire and elsewhere to tell the bees about a death in the family, a custom known as the *Telling of the Bees*, which involved gently tapping on the skep[461] and reciting a charm, *'Bees, bees, awake! Your Master is dead, and another you must take.'* The custom was especially important should the loss be of their primary keeper or the local bee expert, the *Beo Ceorl* ('Bee Master').[462] If the custom was not carried out, it was believed the colony would swarm from the hive or, worse, that another death might follow. Sometimes a black ribbon was also tied around the hive to mark the death[463] and usually, following the death of the Beo Ceorl, no honey would be taken that year.[464]

The New Forest was once renowned for its Old English Mead, or *'medu'*,[465] and local author Irene Soper gives traditional recipes for New Forest meads such as *Sweet Mead* that uses heather honey. *Pyment Mead* (blended with spices) and *Morat Mead* (blended with mulberries) were also popular. Common Mead, such as *Abbots Well Mead* was also made, using honeycomb refuse (the imperfect combs from stripped skeps). This was made by simmering in a pan of rainwater to separate the wax, adding and fermenting yeast, then storing for one year before bottling. Juliette de Bairacli Levy[466] describes how unpopular visitors to the New Forest were given a big glass of this very alcoholic mead before they left, so they would fall off their horses on the way home!

459 Wanderers in the New Forest: Juliette de Bairacli Levy
460 The Pattern Under The Plough: George Ewart Evans
461 The Pattern Under The Plough: George Ewart Evans
462 Hogs at the Honeypot: Frank Vernon
463 The Folklore of Hampshire and the Isle of Wight: Wendy Boase
464 The New Forest, Its Traditions, Inhabitants and Customs: De Crespigney & H Hutchinson
465 John Richard de Capel Wise: The New Forest, Its History & Its Scenery
466 Wanderers in the New Forest: Juliette de Bairacli Levy

THE WILD BOAR

The Wild Boar is the ancestor of our domestic pig, now hunted to the point of extinction. See *'The Hampshire Hog'* for more on the Wild Boar in the Forest and its folklore.

WOLVES, DOGS & WILD CATS

Many are familiar with the legendary Beast of Bodmin and the Hound of the Baskervilles, but it may come as a surprise that the New Forest also has its fair share of spectral cats and phantom dog sightings.

Cat Beasts of the New Forest

Far from being unknown to our British ancestors, the big cat was the subject of travelling tales and folk legend. Indeed the UK had its very own native lynx, once widespread as recently as Roman Britain, but subsequently eradicated by deforestation and persecution.[467] The big cat was the archetypal Cat-Beast; perhaps a folk memory of our native lynx and British wildcat combined with fireside stories of exotic big cats which arrived in travelling menageries[468] or were shipped to Britain as grand gifts for royalty, arriving with golden chains about their necks.

The UK's British wild cat (*Felis silvestris*) is nicknamed the *'Wolf of the Wood'*[469] or the *'British Tiger'*. Although resembling a domestic cat, it has much larger features and has never been tamed (even when hand-reared from a kitten). The wooded areas of the New Forest may well have once been an ideal habitat for the British wild cat, although it is believed that they had been completely eradicated in Hampshire by the 16th century. Due to centuries of persecution and hybridisation with domestic cats, their numbers sadly declined and they are now critically endangered with no known populations in the UK (excluding Scotland). Despite this, even since their presumed extinction occasional sightings have been made all over Britain, proving that

---

467 www.wildlifetrusts.org
468 Roaring Dorset – Encounters with Big Cats: Merrily Harpur
469 Lost Beasts of Britain: Anthony Dent

in some places this animal may have simply endured in the shadows, largely undetected due to its stealthy behaviour and remote habitat. In some cases, the wild cats spotted may be the result of hybridisation with feral domestics,[470] but they are nonetheless as wild as the hills. Hope Bourne writes about his own encounter in the 1940's, in his book *Living on Exmoor*:

> '...*one came slinking down the lane in broad daylight*
> ... *about the size of a dog fox. In colour it was grey or*
> *tawny-grey, marked all over with dark stripes. Its head was*
> *huge in comparison with that of an ordinary cat, and its teeth*
> *protruded below the lip like fangs. Its tail was thick and*
> *blunt ... to a small boy there was something very frightening*
> *in the whole appearance of this remarkable cat.*'[471]

When the wild cat was more numerous, the creature acquired a reputation for taking poultry and even small pets. There were even authenticated reports of wild cats attacking humans[472] (a behaviour unusual to their nature and probably a result of being approached or hunted). But either way, their reputation caused the wild cat to become an ominous creature of folklore: '*Gather up pussy, drive in the chickens, and go inside the house if any such creature approaches the farmyard...*' [473] It is probably fair to say that the reputation of the wild cat was more of a 'Beast' than it was in reality; but this stealthy, elusive creature had already entered British folklore. No doubt conflated with the lynx and black panther of the continent, the archetypal Cat-Beast of the Forest only became larger and more menacing in the British subconscious, and folk tales described its size, prowess and ferocity; he was the *Chat-Loup* ('cat-wolf'), the *Catamount* 'catte of the mountayne'.

The Celtic pixy the *Cait-Sidhe* was probably inspired by the folktales of the *Beast-Cat* of Britain. A fairy spirit or witch, the Cait-Sidhe had the ability to shapeshift into a black cat 'as big as a dog' with white markings (a disconcertingly similar description

---

470 www.gwct.org.uk
471 Living on Exmoor: Hope Bourne
472 Lost Beasts of Britain: Anthony Dent
473 Lost Beasts of Britain: Anthony Dent

to my own cat!) Legend says the Cait-Sidhe can shift into cat form and back eight times but if transformed a ninth time would remain a cat.[474] The Cait-Sidhe was also known to steal the souls of the recently deceased; the belief was so strong that people held deathbed vigils to watch over the body to ensure a cat did not approach the corpse. It was also forbidden to light a fire near the body as the warmth of the flames was known to draw the Cait-Sidhe. Witches shapeshifting into animals such as foxes, hares and cats is a common theme across Britain, and the south coast had its own share of these stories. Jeremy Harte writes of a tale from the nearby Isle of Purbeck, which according to legend was home to a witch named Jinny Gould. She used to spend her nights sat on her garden gate in the form of a cat, terrifying any travellers who passed by.[475] Of course cats have also been used for centuries as agents in counter-witchcraft, their mummified bodies concealed in walls and believed to warn away or fight witch's familiars.[476] The author Robin Young wrote in 1907 about another legendary cat-beast from the south coast, this time in nearby Dorset:

> '*A wild and savage cat, which haunted the remains of the old castle … on Newton Hill … this monster cat, with eyes as big as saucers … not only children but grown-up people would be so afraid that they would walk on the main road below the hill to avoid the creature*.'[477]

For those who inhabited the remotest parts of the British Isles, the fear of big cats was firmly fixed; perhaps today its folklore lives on in modern sightings. Some believe these sightings may be the ancestral memories of those fireside stories, phantom cats of legend or shapeshifting spirits which drift between the worlds. Yet an incredible number of sightings have been reported in Dorset and Hampshire over the last 40 years, with many of the reports made by the most unlikely people. One

---

474 Deborah MacGillivray: Cait Sidhe
475 Jeremy Harte – Luckham, 1906
476 Physical Evidence for Ritual Acts, Sorcery & Witchcraft - 'Concealed Animals'
Brian Hoggard
477 Reminiscences of Sturminster Newton: Robin Young

of the earliest contemporary accounts in the New Forest comes from 1920, when a black cat leapt out in front of two horse riders between Holmsley and Burley, snatching a Jack Russell Terrier.[478] The 1920 black cat sighting would not be the last for the Burley area; later incidents included two sightings at neighbouring properties in Burley, plus another in the vicinity of the Markway and Wilverley inclosures to the south-east of the village. To the east, sightings have been reported at Bolderwood, Ladycross and Slufters, where a black cat was spotted with a deer in its mouth.[479] Further north, a black cat was flushed from the undergrowth by a dog at Godshill and sightings have also been reported at Linford inclosure, Picket Hill and Poulner, Gorley[480] and Rockford.[481]

Hounds of the New Forest

During certain periods of history, the wolf was counted as one of the ancient *Beasts of Venery* in Forest Law; an animal that could be hunted in the Forest, along with others such as deer, wild boar, marten and hare. The New Forest lacks placenames or other significant indications to suggest that wolves once roamed here, however it is more than likely; since they were once prolific in Britain and mentioned in Saxon and Roman records,[482] thriving on remote, open environments such as the New Forest, where there were large numbers of deer and smaller prey. In the wider Hampshire area, wolves are remembered at Woolmer Forest (old Saxon *Wulfmaeres Gemaere*) and Wolvesey (*Wolves' Isle*), where hunters took the heads of wolves to receive their reward.[483]

The wolf would be hunted mercilessly to extinction in the British Isles. Unlike the deer, which were protected against poaching, with strict penalties to preserve their numbers for the King's Hunt, the wolf was hunted largely for the purpose of elimination, to prevent the loss of livestock. In the summer

---

478 Jonathan McGowan, www.thenaturalstuff.co.uk
479 Mike Coggan, Grizzly Productions
480 Roaring Dorset – Encounters with Big Cats: Merrily Harpur
481 Sightings of Big Cats in the Fordingbridge & Surrounding Villages (Facebook Group)
482 Wildlife in Britain & Ireland: Richard Perry
483 A History of Hunting in Hampshire: Brig. Gen. JFR Hope

wolves took smaller game such as mice and voles, but during the winter they would have taken larger prey such as boar, deer and farm animals, which made them a threat to both local farmers and the Crown. As such, the wolf suffered unreserved hunting throughout the UK, being killed by Kings and paupers alike.[484] The method of hunting was generally with dogs or on horseback with poisoned spears; the 1600 tome *Herbal* describes the use of the plant wolfsbane to this effect:

> *'[Wolfsbane] is used among hunters which seeke after wolves ... it is of such force that if any foure footed beast be wounded with an arrow dipped in the juice thereof they die within halfe an houre.*[485]

Together with their night-time visits to farmsteads to prey on farm stock, wolves developed a blood-thirsty reputation in the British subconscious. Some rogue wolves were recorded to have been a danger to humans, and guides gave instruction on how to treat wounds they inflicted, with a particular concern to bites (wolves' teeth or saliva were at one time believed to be venomous). Vervain was recommended as part of the treatment, also used to treat dog bites.[486] The phenomenon of man-eating wolves was particularly prevalent during the 17th and 18th centuries, when wolves were approaching extinction in the UK. Anthony Dent writes how the day before the last wolf was killed (Findhorn, 1743), the wolf in question attacked and killed two schoolchildren in broad daylight.[487] It is probably fair to say that if any of these man-eating wolf reports were true, they were probably the result of the almost total loss of their habitat and their increasing need to take risks to survive.

> *There was a little girl called Little Red Riding Hood, who lived at the edge of a big, dark Forest ... "hello little girl", said the big bad wolf, "are you lost?"*

Wolves were certainly considered to have a firm connection with the chthonic. Associated with death and destruction, the

---

484 The New Forest: Horace Hutchinson
485 Herbal: John Gerard
486 Lost Beasts of Britain: Anthony Dent
487 Lost Beasts of Britain: Anthony Dent

wolf was known for scavenging bodies on the battlefield[488] and conflated with the honouring of the heroic nature of the dead in respect for their sacrifice. '*Wulf*' was an Old English title given as a mark of respect,[489] such as the hero *Beowulf* from the epic of the same name. Their connection to death was compounded by (probably unfounded) tales of them digging up bodies from graveyards, and in some places in Britain where wolves were prolific 'wolf-proof' coffins were built to prevent this posthumous offence. To add to the mystery and fear that surrounded the wolf, another dog-beast had entered folklore and the imagination of the British people; the *Were-Wolf*, a shapeshifting creature which was man by day and wolf by night. As a Royal hunting ground, it is very unlikely the wolf endured in the New Forest for as long as in other wild places in the UK. We don't know when the wolf last roamed the New Forest, but the wolf was completely extinct in Britain by 1760 and in Scotland by 1888.[490]

In both Old Welsh and Old Irish, the term 'wild dog' means wolf. [491] Although the wolf is a very different beast to the dog, it certainly may have contributed to the folklore of its domestic cousin. Whilst the wolf was generally considered a hidden adversary, the dog is the archetypal companion to man, in whatever form it might take, and the spectral Black Dog, a ghostly hound seen all over Britain, is one such beast of legend often described as being 'as big as a wolf'. In folklore, this companionship can appear as either ominous or fortuitous. The earliest sighting of the spectral Black Dog can be found in an Anglo-Saxon chronicle of 1127 accompanying a ghostly phantom hunt:

---

488 Lost Beasts of Britain: Anthony Dent
489 Black Dog Folklore: Mark Norman
490 The Disappearance of Wolves in the British Isles: Ivy Stanmore
491 Lost Beasts of Britain: Anthony Dent

'Many men saw and heard a great number of huntsmen hunting. The huntsmen were black, huge and hideous and rode on black horses and on black he-goats and their hounds were jet black and big-eyed and loathsome.'[492]

As their name suggests, spectral dogs are almost always black. They are also often seen wearing a chain. The fur of the Black Dog is described as being smooth and shiny although bristly to the touch, like a boar's coat; this is a particularly interesting point as Black Dogs are also known for their ability to shapeshift into pigs (amongst other animals including donkeys, crows and goats).[493] The Black Dog is also described as having 'eyes as large as saucers', a phrase shared with the shape-shifting Celtic fairy the *Cait-Sidhe*, which appears as a black cat with white markings. In its malign form the Black Dog is the harbinger of bad omens - a Hellhound, the diabolic agent of the devil; *The Shuck*. He is known to pace highways just as the devil, the ancestral memory of the old chthonic gods, was believed to travel on old trackways. Gemma Gary writes that the *Bucca* (like *Pooke*, also from *Pouke* meaning *'devil'*) was known to traverse the ancient trackways such as the Abbotts Way on a black horse[494] and, closer to home, the road from Silchester to London is known as the 'Devils Highway'. The devil was also held responsible for ditches, such as Grim's Ditch on Breamore Down just to the north-west of the Forest.

In the New Forest, there is also a malevolent canine spirit known as the *shammocking dog*,[495] an idle, thievish dog who is just possibly connected to the imp *Laurence*. However, the Black Dog is also known to be a guardian against malevolence and is often described as having a hand in dispensing justice to wrongdoers by dragging them to hell. There is one well-known New Forest legend which involves the Black Dog doing just this, although the dog is rarely mentioned in most accounts.

This surrounds the death of William II or William 'Rufus' ('Red'). In the run-up to Rufus' death on the 21st of August 1100,

---

492 Westcountry Folklore Symposium 2015
493 Black Dog Folklore: Mark Norman
494 Traditional Witchcraft, A Cornish Book of Ways: Gemma Gary
495 John Richard de Capel Wise: The New Forest, Its History & Its Scenery

several omens predicted his demise. The devil had appeared to several local people, in some cases as a Black Dog foretelling his impending death. Cistercian monks had visions of him being dragged to hell on the back of a Black Dog,[496] in the classic manner of the 'diabolic' Barguest hellhound. Many of these omens reached the King the day before the hunt, during his stay at the Hunting Lodge at Castle Malwood, and the King himself had dreams of streams of blood - but according to legend, defied the warnings. The hunt went ahead as planned and as the evening approached they reached a clearing in the woods - which would be the setting for the Kings' demise. This location is disputed. Popular legend suggests Canterton Glen near Minstead, where the commemorative *Rufus Stone* stands; however other accounts indicate the death was actually near Beaulieu *'in a Beaulieu tract,* [497] close to where his father had destroyed the chapel at Thorougham (a village that no longer exists, but in the general location of Park Farm). A stag was flushed out of the undergrowth in front of the King and what happens next varies from one tale to another. Some say an arrow deflected off the stag whilst others say it was off an old oak tree (since referred to as the *Rufus Oak*). Other accounts describe how it was off a boar (an interesting alternative, which might link with the spectral Black Dog, which is also known to shapeshift into a pig or boar). Either way, the arrow struck the King and he was killed. Everyone fled the scene and Sir Walter Tirel, who absconded to France, was singled out as the likely suspect. The chances are, however, that if it was premeditated murder, it was likely arranged by Rufus' brother Henry who claimed the throne shortly after and buried Rufus with very little ceremony.

The legend continues that a charcoal burner named Purkiss found the body and took him to Winchester in his cart, a trail of blood running behind the cart the whole way. It is said that a Black Dog paces this route following the blood trail of the slain King, classic Black Dog behaviour of patrolling a particular

---

496 The Folklore of Hampshire & the Isle of Wight: Wendy Boase
497 Florence of Worcester

stretch of road and following the deceased. Local folklore also tells that the ghost or *shim* (a local term for ghost) of Rufus is seen riding a Black Dog (or Black Goat) in the New Forest, an echo of the omen foreseen imminently before his death. It is worth noting that in 1100 surnames did not exist and no medieval writers mention a charcoal burner, so this part of the legend is probably a later addition. Incidentally, a cottage near Canterton that was allegedly the home of Purkiss was known to be haunted by a black spirit.[498]

Research into Black Dog legends carried out in the 1960's proved that in many cases, the Black Dog was more often a neutral or even protective entity towards the people it encounters.[499,500] In other cases the dog acts as the archetypal ferryman, transporting or accompanying individuals to their final destination (whether that be a favourable one or an unfortunate one, such as hell). This is reflected in the behaviour reported by sightings and legends; the Black Dog pacing certain stretches of roads, byways and crossroads, accompanying travellers using the route, 'padding along' with them until the traveller walks beyond the limits of the dog's haunt. As such, in some counties the dog is called *'Padfoot'*, referring to the sound of its footfall - or possibly from the Gaelic for 'fairy-dog'.[501] It is also known to haunt liminal places such as riverbanks, bridges and marshes, something it has in common with other local fairy spirits such as the Colt-Pixy and Will-O-the-Wisp. Black Dogs are also seen accompanying spectral carriages, such as on Gorley Road and Ellingham Drove at Rockford in the New Forest. Here, many reports exist of a stagecoach pulled by black horses, with a Black Dog keeping pace. According to folklore, Black Dogs are known to accompany people who are about to die (or were recently deceased), and it has been suggested that the stagecoach is carrying the ghost of Alice Lisle, who was put to death in 1685. She is also said to haunt

498 The New Forest, Its Traditions, Inhabitants and Customs: De Crespigney & H Hutchinson
499 Ethel Rudkin, Ruth Tongue & Theo Brown
500 Black Dog Folklore: Mark Norman
501 Black Dog Folklore: Mark Norman

the nearby Moyles Court School (her former home)[502] and the Alice Lisle pub (although this was formally a primary school, which closed in the 1960's). Another stagecoach accompanied by a Black Dog has been seen at Catherine's Cross in nearby Bridport, where the Black Dog is headless.[503]

It is rare for Black Dogs to be found haunting houses, although not unknown. There is an account of a Black Dog that rushed into a cottage in the New Forest, and then back out again through the walls.[504] This may however be connected to foundation sacrifices and dogs concealed in properties to offer protection to the household. Although dog skeletons are one of the rarer animals found to have been used as concealed charms, out of just five discovered in the UK, two were found in Hampshire and the nearby county of Dorset. One skeleton was found in 1967 at The Crown Hotel in nearby Alton, a building which had previously been haunted by the sound of 'dog-like' scratchings.[505] Another was found at Walnut Farm in Corfe Castle, where a puppy was found beneath the floorboards together with a child's shoe and some 18th-century coins, both classic foundation sacrifices. [506]

---

502 The Folklore of Hampshire & the Isle of Wight: Wendy Boase
503 Mysterious Dorset: Rodney Legg
504 The Folklore of Hampshire & the Isle of Wight: Wendy Boase
505 Physical Evidence for Ritual Acts, Sorcery & Witchcraft– Concealed Animals: Brian Hoggard
506 Physical Evidence for Ritual Acts, Sorcery & Witchcraft– Concealed Animals: Brian Hoggard

CONCLUSION

I sit at my writing desk; the rain driving against the window and watch the autumn leaves start to fall. As the boughs of the great oaks at the end of our garden become bare, I can begin to see past their branches and out to the foggy moor beyond. My little fragment of a world without the rush and intrusion of modern life, nor beholden to the status quo. How easily I could have ended up anywhere else, if not for being gifted this very place by the *genii loci* in one synchronous moment.

Having lived on and around the New Forest my whole life, I have always been aware of the traditions that are alive in this region. Many are in plain sight, but I had always wanted to dig deeper into the accompanying folklore and beliefs which might lie beneath the surface. Suffice to say, I was not disappointed and found a wealth of superstitions, beliefs and old ways that formed the basis of both this landscape and others of a similar nature. Indeed, there are lots of books written about the New Forest, but hardly any at all that discuss its folklore and traditions in detail. Some aspects are even more elusive; their origins forgotten in the mists of time or at the very least unspoken. As the old adage goes, a family should live and work on the Forest for at least three generations before they are considered locals; I suspect the same applies to the knowledge of old Forest lore.

It is so important to retain the intriguing beliefs and practices of this region, which unlike other more documented counties such as East Anglia, is largely shrouded or in danger of being lost altogether. That has been the aim of this book, which I hope may also act as a starting point for future research and, for some, to support and develop practices in the New Forest which are active today.

APPENDICES: FORGOTTEN LANGUAGE OF THE NEW FOREST

I have compiled a list of terms local to the New Forest traditionally used in it and surrounding areas. This is certainly not a complete list and is simply my own collection of phrases. Some I have become familiar with myself from living in the area, others only since researching this book. Although some of these phrases are still in use today, especially those associated with commoning, most are gradually dying out or already been forgotten, other than being listed in antiquated books often difficult to obtain. I hope that by recording some of them here, they will not be forgotten completely.

FORGOTTEN PHRASES: A NEW FOREST GLOSSARY

All in a copse: (saying) Indistinct/confused
An iron windfall: (saying) Anything unfairly taken
Assart: Rooting up woods and to break up for agriculture (offence)
Ball: Area/mound of sand
Blow-up: A pony that suddenly gives up/runs out of steam during the Drift
Bottom: Valley, running between hills or heaths of the Forest
Bowerstone: Boundary Stone
Brize: To press
Brownies: Bees (insect)
Bunny: A gully where a stream flows down to the sea
Bunny Holly/Kind Holly: Holly with fewer prickles/softer leaves
Butts: Tumuli/Barrows
Cassock/Wythwind: Bindweed
Castle: Barrow site
Chalkers: Shoes
Churm: Charm

Clodhopper/Swede Basher: Amusing expression for country dweller

Colt Pixy: Spirit creature who lures ponies and travellers into the bogs

Cord of Wood: Measure of wood (1 'cord' is equal to 4ft x 4ft x 8ft).

Crazy Pates: Marsh Marigold/Kingcup (plant)

Crink Crank: New Forest term for 'nonsense words'. Otherwise used to describe a type of wall, the 'crinkle crankle' (Old English for 'zig-zag')

Crossing the Grids: Leaving the Forest for neighbouring non-Forest districts

Cutty: Wren (bird) also 'Kittywitch'

Deor: Wild Beasts; a place of corpses

Drift/Colt-Hunting: Pony round-up

Droke: Old trackway, from Anglo Saxon 'Drog' to drag/proceed

Drunch: To squeeze

Dykes: Wild Daffodils (plant)

Eat your own side, speckleback: (saying) Reference to greedy people

Emmet: Ant (insect)

Emmet Mound: Grassy hillock containing the nest of Meadow Ants

Estovers, Right of: To gather firewood for fuel

Fairy Line: Natural avenue between rows of trees; usually towards water

Fairy Path: Naturally created pony/deer path across the moors

Fence Month: Period of time during the summer when stock must be brought back into holding land. (now obsolete)

Fire Bladder: A pimple on the face

Flisky Rain: Misty Rain

Flitch: Good-natured

Furze: Gorse (plant)

Fuzzacker: Warbler (bird)

Galley: Signal Fire; to Frighten

Gally Bagger: Scarecrow

Giggle: Any small thing that doesn't stand up straight

Glow Blow: Will-o-the-Wisp

Gold Withy: Bog Myrtle (plant)

Gorgio: Romany term for non-Gypsy

Grockle: Tourist/Outsider

Hat / Hatt: A small tree-crowned hill; clump of trees

Hault Boys: Oak, Beech, Sweet Chestnut, Birch, Yew, Alder, Whitebeam, Ash, Scots Pine, Larch, Spruce, Fir. *'Every tree that doth grow within the Forest, as well that which is called Hault Boys'* See also 'South Boys'

Haunt: An area of the Forest that a herd generally stays within

Head Pegs: Teeth

Heft: Lift

Hefting/Hoofing: A herd visiting the same *Haunts*

Hell: A dark place in the Forest; from *Helan*, 'to cover'

Higgler: A type of Pedlar; a regular but casual seller of goods (such as vegetables) at markets

Hock-Tides: Hock tide money, common in the New Forest until recently

Hoo: Simmer/Boil

Hooi: Whistling of wind, i.e., through a keyhole or round a corner

Huff: Herd of animals

Humwater: Bishopwort Tea / or Horsemint Tea

Jossy Grigory: Nightjar (bird)

Lance: A deer's leap/bound

Laurence: A local fairy/imp who causes laziness 'A Touch of Lawrence' (saying) reference to being lazy

Ledenhall: Empty place

Levancy & Couchancy: 'Animals that rise up and lie down on the land to which the owners' rights attach' (return home/have space to return home)

Like a Swarm of Bees all in a Charm: (saying) To appear under an enchantment; to focus on one specific goal unreservedly, as if under a spell

Ling: Heather (plant)

Louster: Noise, racket

Marl, Right of: To dig clay (Right now obsolete)

Mast, Right of: To turn pigs out on the Forest

Motes/Moots: Roots of Trees

Moore/Moor/More: An area of marsh

Mulloch: Dirt/Soil

Nitch: Bundle of kindlewood

Onion: A local giant responsible for hurling stones

Ooser: An entity with cattle-like features who reprimands wrong-doing

Over Runner: A shrew mouse. If it runs over your shoe its bad luck

Pannage: See Mast, Right of

Passage: Fire break or ford

Pasture, Right of: To graze cattle, ponies and occasionally sheep

Perambulation: Outer boundaries of the New Forest

Picked Piece: A field with sharp, angular corners

Plock: Block (of wood)

Pole: Head

Polly Dishwasher: Wagtail (bird)

Pound: Enclosures on the Forest used to temporarily hold stock

Purpresture: Encroachment onto the Forest by building or enclosure (offence)

Pricking: To ride to/ride in a Hunt

Rattle like a boar in a holme bush: (saying) To excessively talk; rattle on

Reremouse: Bat

Rick-Rack: Stormy, windy weather

Rides: Green passageways between or running around inclosures

Ronge: Ponies kicking in play

Scroop: A creaking sound

Shade: A breezy spot on the New Forest where the ponies and cattle traditionally congregate to take respite from the flies

Shim: Thin person; sometimes used to refer to a Ghost

Sheets Axe: Oak Apple (plant)

Shoots: Hills (such as Red Shoot of red sand and White Shoot of white sand)

Sinking Mud: Bog

Smoke Pennies: Payment made for Turbary (now obsolete)

Sniggle: Species of eel (*anguilla mediorostris*)

South Boys: Holly, Thorn, Crab-Apple, Sallow, Furze, Bog Myrtle, Spindle, Dogwood, Juniper. See also 'Hault Boys'

Spith: Strength/Force

Squoyling/Squirrel Snodding: Hunting squirrels

Squoyle: A mean glance, or to slander (from Squoyling Squirrels)

Stools: Stumps of trees
Stout/Gadfly: Horsefly or Crabfly (Note: the word 'horse' also used locally to mean 'large')
Swain: Freeholder
Swathe/Swaeth: Track through the Forest
Three Cunning: Reference to a shrewd person or animal
Trail: Flowers on an oak
Treader: Bicycle
Turbary, Right of: To dig peat for fuel (right now obsolete)
Vert: Woods, 'herbage' and undergrowth
Venery: Beasts of the Hunt
Waste: To cut down/clear trees (offence)
Weet Bird: Wryneck (bird)
Wickering: Young pony neighing
Winter Heyning: Period of time during the winter when stock must be brought back into holding land. (now obsolete)
Wood Findey Rain: Persistent rain from the South-East /rain that lasts all day
Yaffingale/Wood Knocker: Green Woodpecker (bird)

SOME LOCAL NAMES AND THEIR POSSIBLE MEANINGS

Boldre: River marked by rushes; or 'by the flat-topped hill'

Bramshaw: Bramble bush, or Broom

Bransgore: *'gore'* meaning triangular piece of land

Bratley: Brittle clearing/wood

Breamore: Broom covered marsh or moor

Brockenhurst: Broken wooded hill, or badger wood

Brook: Streamside meadow

Burley: Fortified wood/clearing

Cadnam: 'Cada's Estate' – Cada from *'catu'* meaning battle

Calmore: Cabbage marshland; possibly reference to Sea Kale

Canterton: 'Farm of the Kentish men'

Copythorne: Pollarded hawthorn

Crow: A ford, stepping stones or hovel

Dibden: Valley by deep water

Dockens Water: Dark/Secluded water

Eyeworth: Yew weir or fish-pond, or streamside/marsh

Fawley: Fallow wood/clearing

Fordingbridge: Bridge of the dwellers at Ford

Fritham: Scrub on the edge of the Forest/cultivated plot on marginal land

Gorley: *'gore'* meaning triangular piece of land

Hale: Nook, angle

Hanger: Sloping wood

Holbury: Moated site

Hordle: Treasure hoard/hill. May be associated with barrows/haunted places

Ibsley: 'Tibb's wood/clearing'

Ipley: Clearing with hunting platform

Lepe: Leaping place for deer; jumpable stream or crossing place

Linford: Ford by the lime tree

Lyndhurst: Lime wood

Matley: Wood where rushes (for matts) were obtained

Minstead: Place where mint grew

Mockbeggar: A house or farm where no welcome will be found

Netley Marsh: Wet wood

Ower: Flat-topped ridge, or bank of slope

Pennington: Penny farm, a farm which a penny geld was payable

Pilley: Wood where shafts or piles are obtained, or Tidal creek

Plaitford: Ford where games took place

Poulner: Bank/slope, or flat-topped ridge and reference to Pennyroyal (plant)

Ringwood: Border/edge

Rockford: Rooks Ford (the Ford over Dockens Water) *Rakfordesbrook*

Setley: Planted wood/stunted

Sopley: From 'Soc Leag' land that held a court of *socmen* (tenants)

Sway: Track through the Forest/Sow enclosure

Warborne: Stream with weirs and fish traps

Wellow: 'Pale colour of fermenting milk' possible reference to River Blackwater

List compiled largely from Sue Davies, Karen Walker & Linda Coleman's 'The New Forest Historical Landscape', with thanks.

Bibliography

Ackroyd, Peter: The History of England VI

Allies, J.: On the Ignis Fatuus

Anon: Gipsy Missioning in the New Forest, 1934

Apperson, George L: Dictionary of Proverbs

Aubrey, John: The Natural History of Wiltshire

Barnes, Rev. W: Glossary of Dorset

Birks, Johnny: Pine Martens

Boase, Wendy: The Folklore of Hampshire & the Isle of Wight

Boel, Geoff: Picturesque Pubs of the New Forest

Bourne, Hope: Living on Exmoor

Bracelin, Jack: Gerald Gardner, Witch

Bramshaw, Vikki: Craft of the Wise

Brunskill, RW: Illustrated Handbook of Vernacular Architecture

   ---------: Traditional Buildings of Britain

Champion, Matthew: Medieval Graffiti

Clebert, Jean Paul: The Gypsies

Cleere & Nurney: Nightjars

Cox, Nicolas: The Gentleman's Recreation

Croker, Thomas C: Fairy Legends & Traditions of the South of Ireland

Cuttriss, Frank: Romany Life

d'Este, Sorita & Rankine, David: Isles of the Many Gods

Dacombe, Marianna: Dorset Up-Along and Down-Along

Davies, Sue & Walker, Karen & Coleman, Linda: The New Forest Historical Landscape

De Crespigny, Rose & Hutchinson, Horace: The New Forest, Its Traditions, Inhabitants and Customs

D.E. Jenkins: Bedd Gelert: Its Facts, Fairies & Folklore

Dent, Anthony: Lost Beasts of Britain

Dobell, Horace: Medical Aspects of Bournemouth and its Surroundings

Duignan, Marie: National Folklore Collection of Ireland (Coolronan School)

Evans, George Ewart: The Pattern Under The Plough

Farrar, Janet & Russell, Virginia: The Magical History of the Horse

Farrar, Janet and Stewart: The Witches' God

Gardner, Gerald: The Meaning of Witchcraft

Gary, Gemma: Traditional Witchcraft, A Cornish Book of Ways

Gerard, John: Herbal

Gibbins, Henry: Gipsies of the New Forest

Gilpin, William: Remarks on Forest Scenery

Goff, Gerald L: History of Hale

Griffin, Emma: Blood Sport - Hunting in Britain since 1066

Griffith, RWS: The Gipsies of the New Forest – Field Meeting 1893

Grimassi, Raven: Encyclopaedia of Wicca & Witchcraft

Groves, Nicholas: Devil's Doors Revisited

Harpur, Merrily: Roaring Dorset – Encounters with Big Cats

Harte, Jeremy: Luckham, 1906

Heath, Sidney H: Parts of a Cottage

Heselton, Philip: In Search of the New Forest Coven

----------: Wiccan Roots

Hoggard, Brian: Magical House Protection, The Archaeology of Counter-Witchcraft

----------: Physical Evidence for Ritual Acts, Sorcery & Witchcraft - 'Concealed Animals'

----------: Archaeology of Ritual & Magic (Zoom Lecture 18.04.20)

Hope, Brig. Gen. JFR: The History of Hunting in Hampshire

Hope, Robert Charles: The Legendary Lore of the Holy Wells of England

Hoskins, WG & Dudley Stamp, L: The Common Lands of England and Wales

Hutchinson, Horace: The New Forest

Hutton, Ronald: The Pagan Religions of the Ancient British Isles

Jacob, Grimm,: Teutonic Mythology

James, Jude: East Boldre, A New Forest Squatters Settlement

----------: Vernacular Architecture in the New Forest (Hampshire Field Club report no. 15)

Journal of the Derbyshire Archaeological & History Society, 1907

Katherine Oldmeadow: The Folklore of Herbs

Kemp, Richard: Some Apotropaic Marks in the church of St Mary the Virgin, Fordingbridge

Kenchington, FE: The Commoners New Forest

Knight, Peter: Ancient Stones of Dorset

Larwood, J & Hotton, J: The History of Signboards

Leek, Sybil: Diary of a Witch

Legg, Penny: Folklore of Hampshire

Legg, Rodney: Mysterious Dorset

Levy, Juliette de Bairacli: Wanderers in the New Forest

Leyland, Charles Godfrey: Gypsy Sorcery & Fortune Telling

Light, Anthony & Ponting, Gerald: The Saxon Church of Breamore

Loktionov, Alex: A Ritualistic Interpretation of Bronze-Age Burnt Mounds

MacGillivray, Deborah: Cait Sidhe

Manwood, John: Manwood's Treatise of the Forest Laws (1598)

McNair, Dionis: New Forest Ponies

Mellinkoff, Ruth: Averting Demons

Millais, John G: British Deer & their Horns

Millson, Cecilia: Tales of Old Hampshire

Monaghan, Patricia: Changeling Cattle & Magical Cows

New Forest National Park Authority: Cultural Heritage of the New Forest

Norman, Mark: Black Dog Folklore

Papworth, Martin: The Search for the Durotriges

Pasmore, AH & Pallister, J: Boiling Mounds in the New Forest

Pasmore, Anthony: New Forest Pottery Kilns & Earthworks

----------: New Forest Notes (Lymington Times September 1994)

----------: Verderers of the New Forest

Pasmore, Hugh: A New Forest Commoner Remembers

Paultons Romany Museum: Romany Life & Customs

Peckham, B&G: Churches of the New Forest

Pennick, Nigel: Secrets of East Anglian Magic

Perambulation 1215 Christchurch Cartulary (Christopher Tower Library)

Perry, Richard: Wildlife in Britain & Ireland

Perry, W: A Treatise on the Identity of Herne's Oak

Porteous, Alexander: The Forest in Folklore & Mythology

Pulman, George: The Book of the Axe

Readers Digest Book of British Birds

Reeves, Richard: Linwood Searchlight Site, New Forest Knowledge archive

----------: New Forest Hauntings

Richard de Capel Wise, John: The New Forest, Its History & Its Scenery

Roberts, Edward: Hampshire Houses 1250-1700 (contribution by Linda Hall)

Robins, Frederick: The Smith

Sayce, RU: The One Night House & its Distribution (Folklore Journal, 1942)

Scarre, Chris: Timeline of the Ancient World

Schneidau, Lisa: Woodland Folk Tales of Britain and Ireland

Sibley & Fletcher: Discovering the New Forest

Sikes, Wirt: British Goblins

Smith, Ian: Romany Nevi-Wesh

Soper, Irene: New Forest Cookery – Traditional Recipes from a New Forest Cabin

----------: The Romany Way

----------: My New Forest Home

----------: The Romany Way

Stagg, DJ: Calendar of New Forest Documents 15th-17th centuries (Perambulation 1670)

Stanmore, Ivy: The Disappearance of Wolves in the British Isles

Sumner, Heywood: A Winter Walk in the New Forest

----------: The Ancient Earthworks of the New Forest

----------: Cuckoo Hill, The Book of Gorley

----------: The Book of Gorley

----------: The New Forest

The Apophthegmes of Erasmus, 1531

The Compleat Horseman, 1711

The Helm Dictionary of Scientific Bird Names

Thorpe, Benjamin: Northern Mythology

Timbs, John: Knowledge for the People

Valiente, Doreen: Witchcraft for Tomorrow

Vernon, Frank: Hogs at the Honeypot

Wedeck, Harry: Dictionary of Gypsy Life & Lore

West, Ian: Geology of the New Forest (Southampton University)

Wise, JR: The New Forest, its History & its Scenery

Yonge, Charlotte: An Old Woman's Outlook in a Hampshire Village

Young, Robin: Reminiscences of Sturminster Newton

Index

www.avaloniabooks.com